Gallery Books
Editor Peter Fallon

COLLECTED

Seán Dunne

COLLECTED

Edited by Peter Fallon

Gallery Books

Collected
is first published
simultaneously in paperback
and in a clothbound edition
on 8 December 2005.

The Gallery Press
Loughcrew
Oldcastle
County Meath
Ireland

ISBN 1 85235 394 5 *paperback*
     1 85235 395 3 *clothbound*

A CIP catalogue record for this book
is available from the British Library.

Contents

*for Gavin, Eoghan and Niamh
and in memory of Merlin*

Prayer

King of Sunday, guard the wells
and streams. Preserve the woods.

King of Monday, guard the cry
of corncrakes in a mown meadow.

King of Tuesday, let live the frail
petals in limestone landscapes.

King of Wednesday, spare the thin
grass where herds of reindeer feed.

King of Thursday, care for the low
cries of field mice after harvest.

King of Friday, care for the surge
of salmon beneath a Corrib bridge.

King of Saturday, attend the birds:
oiled wings flapping; their clogged throats.

(1993)

Suir Song

Bordered by banks of blackberry and fern,
I plumbed with my father for fish in pools.
Minnows eluded my spread fingers, then
wriggled in my palm like notes uncurled
from the script of an ancient tune:
sweet Suir flow softly till my song's end.

Later I learned of dredged hoards, leavings
of longboats, sword and amulet hauled
from fathoms caked with clinging shells.
Fastened to tides, I heard Sitric stir
light as an insect among reeds:
sweet Suir flow softly till my song's end.

I lay for hours with an ear to the strict
cadence of water, measuring its rhythms
that broke in consort against my boat.
Immersed in that music, I felt clouds
create a slow counterpoint:
sweet Suir flow softly till my song's end.

Spenser's 'Gentle Shure, that making way
by sweet Clonmell, adornes rich Waterford',
its course curved like a thigh when I ran
through fields for its source, that dodged
like the answer to an old riddle:
when found it sang my childhood's end.

(1980)

Message Home

Curving past wards, lawns and avenues teem
with patients strolling to lessen time.
The strands of your hair are split like fine
tweezers as you stand, I imagine, beside
curtains the colour of leaves that fall
on wet pavements near a girls' school.

Here, the valley presents a picture of peace —
an ordered landscape of tranquil fields,
barley broken by the flight of crows
startled by shotguns. Tired of the old
scene, I read Mother Julian in her cell:
each page a promise that all shall be well.

But we inhabit a harsher world, our
lives confined to balconies for an hour
absorbing the sun to lessen our hurt.
A farmer walks acres of turned earth
in the distance, appraising each neat lap.
He walks without watching a sinking graph.

Crows flock in thousands here at night,
each dipping towards its own nest despite
darkness gathering in a sky that's scaled
like a mackerel. Somewhere, in terrible pain,
a man screams, *delirium tremens*, dark
birds enlarge in his mind to a roar.

To cope with such pain I pretend you stand
shelling peas into a white bowl, your hand
deftly tossing pods aside. Or your hair
in a peasant scarf as you prepare
dough on a floured table. Like secrets I set
such pictures against this place where death

is habitual as morning. Wheeled trolleys tell
of another gone, sheets replaced and all
the charts unclipped. The priest towels
chrism from his hands and prays aloud.
I think of you sleeping, your tired face,
banishing the hurt of these times, this place.

Charts

I A HOSPITAL BREAKFAST

The clatter of trolleys draws us out —
the hunched farmer shuffling in a daze
of Mogadon, calling a lost sheepdog.
Or the man who thinks he's Brian Boru,
wary of the blond boxer whose eyes

are swollen and bloodshot from booze.
Here there's nothing to lose, a crude
equality of the lost or mad. Swaying
over toast, a sailor swigs dreamt beer
and sings out of tune to a mate, drowned.

We swallow pills like a final course.
Smooth sweets, they slip from bottles
bright as beads from a toy necklace.
Held between teeth, capsules dissolve.
Chewed, they could be sweetcorn or pastilles.

2 NIGHT LIGHT

Light through windows shifts across
our lockers lined with keepsakes — cracked
photographs, flowers wedged in a vase,
cards from a surprised sister.
If I close my eyes they barely linger.

Over one bed a bulb glows in the night,
a hollow of care for the man
who cringes before the savage rats.
A silver basin lies near his soiled
shirt and trousers crumpled in a chair.

Like a child reading by torchlight, I
turn your picture for the best-lit view.
Framed by moonlight, you smile and wave
from a pier we visited. Beside you I stare
back at myself: Narcissus wary of the pool.

Interior Design

On floors so many others called their own
we spread rush matting and wash borders clean.
Our window in its ring of damp holds a view
they too must have loved — old walls where pairs
of pigeons croon on sills. Our watching makes it new.
We've banished ghosts and discarded the stained
mats, the dated calendars. Crevices already
contain our memory like a fresh paint. Our bed
holds the centre, a lush patchwork you've sewn.
Our imagined children hide acorns in its folds.

The Bean Feast

Stacked in jars on shelves, the beans
diminish in time to favourite recipes.
Poured into bowls, the chosen piles
soak overnight. They burst in darkness
as we sleep, immune to their protest.
As if for a birth, they crack and swell
in cupboards among crockery and herbs.
They soften into life without a sound.

Their names contain them like gloves:
red kidney beans, skins open and loose,
or mung beans, pellets of hard seed.
The blackeye watches us behind glass
and butter beans are smooth as cobbles.
The speckled pinto, the round haricot —
stones for jewellery, pebbles or beads.
The kitchen answers to their every need.

What if they hear us at night, our low
whispers aching for comprehension, sighs
they yearn to decipher? Old favourites
of the earth, they have little to learn.
At times I sense them soaking in the dark,
swelling towards the glimmer of moonlight
between hinges of the pantry door. Cold
multitudes, they absorb our lives as well.

Monet at Giverny

Look at light falling on waterlilies!
They flow in shoals beneath the footbridge
where irises, slender as geisha girls, stiffen
as he approaches at dawn. Shafts
of sunlight strain across acres of haystacks.
Like a harvester he carries a wrapped lunch pack,
his mind swirling with a canvas
that catches each instant of changing light.

Tonight, he'll return to rooms where shelves
are blue playgrounds of hanging delft. Maids
will bustle around him, chattering as they stoke
the fire among smells from the garden.
Shadows will stir in the rucks of Alice's blouse
and again he'll measure the pose of hands
relaxed in her lap or drawing a thread
through linen alive with lamplight.

But now it is time for haystacks and the maze
of light that holds each parched bundle.
They pose like restless models, keen
to assume a different stance and blend
with clouds in colours that challenge his brush.
Cigarettes burn to stubs in his mouth, his hands
harden with caked paint and reek of oil.
His frilled cuffs dampen as the canvas lightens.

The Studio at Shanagarry

for Paul Mosse

The smell of roasted coffee clings
like an extra oil to the still studio.
Canvases against walls, each crisp
completeness held like a breath.
A bluebottle writhes in a white
tray of acid, its wings
sizzling as we talk.
A retriever barks in the yard below.

Otherwise books, brushes, crammed
sketchbooks, palettes, and a cracked
plate among suds in the basin, even
curtains caught in a certain fold.
Here, I am an intruder as these
give way to the fall of shadow
on a stove, or to sunlight's
entrance, an expected guest.

The Quilt Story

for Patricia Cockburn

For years she's been making the quilt,
gathering the clothes her family outgrow.

When her husband died his shirts became
bundles waiting in baskets for the quilt
to absorb them into its diamond world.

In this house nothing is wasted, no jars
thrown out, no object dispensed with.
In time all waste is useful or antique.

And so the quilt grows, a maze to include
old scarves and caps, the ironed lining
of jackets that smell of cigars.

In small squares cut shirts are set
like tesserae in a quilt mosaic, each
square a single story from her life.

There is the sober check of her husband,
the after-school denim of her sons.
There are pieces of blouse and trouser-end,
the cuffs and collars of a work shirt.
Cut any smaller they'd seem like relics.

It grows farther away and longer as she sews,
stretching across the floor piece by piece,
quilt stories, autobiographies, each patch a deed.

Perhaps one night she'll lay it on the bed,
a long parade of fashion in the dark.
Lying under it, she'll hear the flap

of laundry on the line in her garden,
her own clothes drying, and she'll lie
and wonder at the waste of it when she goes.

She will leave her quilt behind like a farm,
her life sewn into its every seam.

The Basket

It cradles coloured hills of wool,
piled among needles and the creased
patterns for clothes you knit

between children asleep and the screen
diminishing to a dot at closedown.
It creaks when I draw it towards you.

Its reeds crackle like sparks,
small detonations when my fingers press.
Moses might have floated in it, adrift

and swaddled on a stream near girls
who pass with pitchers for the well.
Or it might have carried turf, ethnic

and antique, prominent in a postcard
of a Galway bog in the last century,
a shawled girl staring at a camera on stilts.

We might have used it for our yelling sons,
set them inside like prophets
padded in eiderdown, downstream and asleep.

But it lacks the luxury of myth,
resting with its wools piled like skulls
in the corner of a catacomb,

the needles clacking as you concentrate.
So ordinary there is little to be said for it —
it remains a wool basket. It creaks and holds.

Anniversary

One year dead tonight and still no sign
of a comeback, no new recital of the lost
lore and recipes you took when you died.
The last Mills & Boon books I gave you rest
in drawers lined with newspapers,
racing results and pictures of presidents
toppled long since in televised coups.
With them you are a speck in history, too.

One year dead tonight and no one tells
of the doctor falling for the swooning nurse,
his stethoscope twitching near her heart.
For years you read nothing else, except
The Sacred Heart Messenger and *Ireland's Own*.
Your only cosmetic was Eau de Cologne.
You sprayed it at the air like insecticide
to hide smells; polishing made you tired.

One year dead tonight and I think
of your aprons, the bread you baked,
hairnets and coats, your Sunday missal.
In a city hospital before you died you turned
from offered water and asked for the pure
drop from a well you'd known since a girl.
'I'm finished,' you whispered near the end.
You were even too tired for love stories then.

Lament from Another Room

My dead love,
   without permission
they came and washed you
   soaped away your usual smells
dressed you in foolish brown
   despite your love for blue
sadfacedly sat with you
   our private sofa seized
cards scattered around you
   flowers in borrowed bowls
your plants dead on windowsills
   your frozen hands joined
to prevent our further touch
   bass rosaries droned
despite your need for everyday song
   darkly they coffined you
hammered nails into you
   who feared forced things
while rooms away I loved you
   caught gestures in photographs
life in remembered voice
   to spite the dark intruders
with untrammelled song.

Doorsteps

Lovely the women of suburbs in summer,
sitting on doorsteps to talk in the sun,
with their hairdos and magazines on lives of the famous
and their children amok in the gardens.

They talk of old times as they gather,
of girls in their heyday at party and dance
when love was a brightness of seasides in summer
and promises flowed easily as waves.

But now there are daughters who need telling off
for wearing loud clothes and coming home late,
and lately their husbands have fought with their sons
for going away weekends and answering back.

Lovely the women of suburbs in summer,
sitting on doorsteps to talk in the sun,
with their hairdos and magazines on lives of the famous
and the halls of their future behind them.

Suburban Gardener

There's a greenhouse of plastic stretched
over curved rods: his private tropics
where tomatoes ripen and swell.

There are rows of thick-leaved cabbages.
He hacks them from stalks with firm
proprietary strength.

On days of misery and wet he sits
behind lace and watches the showers descend.
His patch is narrowing. All this will end.

Grandparents

They stand at the door
like figures in a weather house,
waving to their children's cars.

If he goes first she'll protest
against help, hating the need,
lost among his unused things,
forgetting to bake for visitors.
Suds will never loosen her rings.

And if she goes he'll proclaim
independence, strictly his own man,
yet attend to room with her methods.
On Sundays he'll snooze among grandchildren,
telling worn jokes, afraid to spill soup.

Limbo

i.m. Seán Ó Ríordáin

Everything was reduced to words.
The noise of feet in wards at night
became syllables of prayer or a sound

soft as slippers on carpet, the quiet
displacement of kindling by fire.
Silence was a vowel, a frozen cloth on briars

stiff as a dead woman's face. Or a lost
language, the stillness in villages
on islands he'd sailed to, keen as Columbus.

Death came like a mother calling early
to the school gates, warm coat in hand
to ease his cold fever, her voice a balm,

her face calm as a countrywoman met at a well.
Until she came he begged air for breath.
Words broke like birds flushed out from fields.

West Cork

for Seán Lucy

1 GOBNAIT'S BED

Cluttered as a bedside table —
the saint's bed strewn with offerings
from hairclips to the crutch of a man
who walked out the gate he'd stumbled
through. Pinned by stones, petitions
flap fiercely as moth wings in a jar.

2 RAG-TREE

Its branches drip with tatters.
It seems held down with pleas.
Over fields it might
be a monster disturbed in a story,
rustling its rags in unease.

3 HOLY WELL

The same tin cup for years but the rim
never spread the hurt that touched it.
Coins glitter in its depths like foil.
The water shivers at the mildest gust.
Pinched by midges, it trembles slightly.

Helvick

Walking the coast road to Helvick,
I remembered teachers calling to cottages,
their heavy bicycles whirring towards words.
Eager at firesides, they trapped sounds
as if words were hares about to slip.

Everywhere revolt shook the burgeoning
state; guns smuggled to a tense coast,
noise besides rain in the fields at night.
In the College, town children prayed
in accents awkward as their unworked hands.

Birds stirred beside me in hedges, as if
to insist that more than the lost be heard.
Walking the coast road to Helvick,
I caught the slurred song of the last traditional
singer, his eyes shut tight as if in pain.

Morning at Mount Melleray

Woken for lauds, I lie
listening to water in the guesthouse garden.
Birdsong chips at the silence.
A gun barks to scare crows from fields.
The morning bell of Melleray booms
over hills where fog thickens.

In the next county you sleep in a house
high over cliffs and a packed harbour.
Perhaps our son is crying, his frail
fists boxing the air until you arrive,
breast-offering, warm, your cheek
flushed where it pressed the pillow.

A monk reads in the long refectory.
Jugs of milk on wooden tables,
plates of bread and cut cheese —
you would like such ordinary scenes
where the clatter of plates is praise,
each movement charged with meaning.

More spectator, voyeur, I kneel in doubt
before the altar. A tabernacle shaped
like a honeycomb gleams under sodium light.
The air is cold as Christ on a crucifix,
his silver legs bent and thin to my touch.
Brown as nuts, beads dangle from fingers.

In farmyards monks scrape dung from drains.
Cylinders turn in the laundry and sheets
are pressed between rollers. Monks slide
wood towards a chainsaw, shavings
spit and snarl around hands.
Poring over books, a novice jots notes.

Here I am learning the meaning of love:
your absence a contact some never know.
Gentle as drizzle, you move in my memory,
your brush daubing a canvas for the true
image you intuit at the heart of paint.
I sense that image in the silence now.

A monk at morning on a long walk talks
of Eliot's rose garden and chances missed.
I sense that door ajar, and you
waiting among the roses, fingers pressed
against petals of the *rosa mundi*.
Briars tangle the chances we failed to take.

In a long shed heavy with potato smells,
I touch and measure the miraculous bin.
Crowds called during famine and were fed
meal until it flowed from tin
basins broken with rust, or poured
from aprons laden like hammocks of grain.

The bin never emptied, but its flow
filled those who walked for days
over mountainsides stifled by famine.
I hear them talking in Irish, all
keen to tell of the miracle at Melleray,
and I know how they felt at such abundance.

I ask for success in simple things:
husbandship and father care, the deep
patience of the monk with ancient texts
that blur and clear with meaning at last.
Everything has the sense of something planned,
nothing is random or out of hand,

insect and animal assume their places.
A speck climbs its Everest stalk.
The air at evening is meshed with midges.
The abbey cat drops an offering at my feet,
a dead bird, then guiltily walks away.
Fish dart and glitter in a fountain pool.

On a pathway in sunlight I think
of the need for gentleness in our affairs.
Water sprays from spinning nozzles as I walk,
drenching the parched vegetables.
I share that need with resurgent roots.
The refreshed stalks strengthen and grow.

Dear heart, our lives unroll like scrolls.
Lectio ends with the shutting of books.
Softly, women confess as shutters slide.
Old pain subsides and wounds are healed.
Stealing from the bakery, odours of bread.
I want to take your hands in mine and press.

Baking Bread

Today you mastered the making of bread,
set raisins in dough like eyes
and mouth on a flattened head.
Straight-faced, we accept your burnt
crisp offering, pleasing you with praise
that seems approval of your ways.

Crumbling in a blackened tin,
your baked bread is startling as a new
word to capture concepts in.
Tomorrow it goes to birds, gulls
hovering scared as you point and shout,
raisins in your hand like eyes plucked out.

Bathtime

for Gavin

Shaping elephants in the suds
you trace a trunk and bellow.
     My practised talk is dull
compared to this tracery, so
much yours it needs nothing of mine.
     This, on paper, suits me fine.

But deep down, it means at last
you start to grow away, to turn
     from my help towards your own path.
Suddenly a future waits where you spurn
my hand before you cross the road.
     This moment lessens both our loads.

Coastal Village, Sunday Night

It might be a picture from emigrant songs —
the harbour packed with trawlers and lines
of net and lobster pots on the swept pier.
Cliffs that stretch either side enfold
the scene like arms, hugging it close
from gales that spin a gull in flight.
The lighthouse beams its warning across
waves that wash against buoys and rocks.

Our dream of life at easy pace
resting in cottages above the sea,
gardens ablaze with flowers, and silence
broken only by our talk. A gnome
is hammering shoes on a gatepost,
his sole purpose to be there. Our need
for the perfect in each state
eludes his patient, weathered gaze.

Brief moonlight frames a passing car
making for home along the coast, or
coves where lovers behind windscreens watch
the break of surf on shingle, the slight
movement of shadows across a headland's tip.
A chip van near the closed pub sends
its smells like signals into homes, warm
odours that blend with salt and fish.

The choice as always rests between
failure or fulfilment of the dream,
lovers caught in the momentary, stark
glare of the lighthouse breaching the dark,
an old bus rumbling through the early hours
with crowds from discos in distant towns.
Together, tired, perhaps they wish
that life more often resembled this.

Tramore

for Des Gloster

Ladies in retouched holiday postcards
step giggling to rows of bathing huts
in the solid blare of a brass band.
Boys, trapped in time, roll stilled hoops.
Gentlemen with canes stroll to sand dunes,
talking of Redmond or the imminent war,
eyeing the picnics of Ursuline schoolgirls.
The sun forever gleams on their watch chains.

Faraway bonfires gleam on the Doneraile.
Centuries ago, a ship sank to such flames,
The Sea Horse stumbling slowly into waves,
officers' white wigs afloat in coves
where waves break across my silence now.
Couples carouse beneath the grey memorial
plaque, filling the cold air with hit songs,
clatter of bottles passed around again.

Miles out at sea I catch the silent glow
of a trawler making for herring grounds:
a glow-worm glistening in the massive dark.
Disc jockeys pile amplifiers onto vans; last
bonfires gutter on clifftops. Now it all
comes down to this — the silence closing in
like the curled corners of a burning photograph,
depicting the last, frail fragments of peace.

Refugees, 1969

They swarmed South in trains and stayed
for weeks in a disinfected barracks.
The word 'refugee' failed to fit those
who walked around Waterford in salvaged clothes,
or idled on benches chewing at matchsticks.
One scaled the side of a handball alley,
threatening to leap into our local abyss.

Others fought in chip shops or went on the piss
in pubs where nothing moved faster than clock hands.
They were far from faces in a flickering crowd
streaming from ghettoes as sirens wailed,
or women stumbling from a bombed hotel
waving bundles to a welcome of flashbulbs.
These were like ourselves. When they left
we waved like exiles from a boat drawing out.

Emigrant Sheds, Cobh

Bricked-up toilets or sealed huts,
the emigrant sheds crumble on piers.
In prints they are thronged with whole
families thin from famine. Over years

they yield to dodgems and arcades,
discos blaring over waves in the dark.
The tin schedules rust in the rain.
The promised land advances towards them.

The Fifth Beatle

Often I dream of you alive, an old joke
in a Hamburg basement where Beatles'
oldies spin nostalgia. The air
is heavy as cotton with joint-smoke.
Dodging mirrors, you douse
your face in the washroom and swear.
Your name avoids our graffiti.

Always someone has to lose, and you
lost more than most. In Munich still
crowds argue on coaches from Dachau,
claim the camp's a slur and deny
the full accounts, the ovens and labs,
newsreels of corpses stacked on slabs.
Against that, what chance have you

who made no more than music? You live
only in footnotes and shaky footage,
a curious appendage to the other four,
forever on the fringe of a dead future
where credits never carry your name
and fans refuse your memory. True
to form, they'll say we invented you.

The Ghetto Women

The scarved women, suitcases held with belts
from overcoats that hung behind doors
of ordinary rooms in another lifetime.
If I dwell on them now it's with the guilt
of one who watches them only in photographs,
or in cinemas where they sob to the sound
of amplified music above train wheels turning.

Their children cling to them as if this
is no more than a visit to the dentist.
After it, there will be twists of liquorice
or coloured cards with pictures of clowns.
Their husbands have long ago disappeared,
their heads shaved, their clothes marked
with triangles stitched in a fatal theorem.

Holding my son's hand on the way to school
I think of them travelling over countrysides,
hemmed in in wagons, too sullen to sing.
Guards measure their shapes from watchtowers.
When I stop to point out trains or to buy
fresh fruit for a lunch bag, I feel his palm
press against mine in a mild excitement.

View from Outside the Fence

They might be monks in a field,
breaking the earth like a crust of bread.
The stack behind them rising through trees
is the bakery where hosts are pressed.

They might be peasants posing for a canvas,
amused by the artist who thinks them authentic.
Their hands are bleeding from briars.
Their clogs are caked in mud and cracking.

They are prisoners clearing ground
for cells they'll inhabit in time,
thinking of home villages or songs
that take them from the task to when

they cleared gardens for vegetables,
their children walking with armfuls of bread,
their wives singing as buckets brimmed.

Quakers

Silence takes over the room.
As if gathered for a sign, they dispatch
business and let the moments pass.
On tables, in bowls, flowers bud
like phrases about to be said.

Outside, their acre of graves
shows names and dates like the flat
covers of shut files. Terraces close
around them, dogs restless in yards,
children at windows catapulting birds.

Against the Storm

War gathers again and the stern
generals argue over outspread maps.
Bullets shatter the high
pulpit where a prelate pleads.
Ministers rant on platform until
words discard meaning and collapse.
Everywhere unease spreads like rumour.

Before it was the same, and small
signals went unnoticed in the dark.
The gross cloud changed nothing despite
the thronged chambers, the skin
shed like a stocking in the bomb's wake.
Afterwards, the cafes opened and stark
lessons were unlearned. Unreal and loud,
laughter drowned the warnings calling

urgent as the cry of a trapped hare.
In spite of headlines now I catch
the stir of my sleeping son
turning to begin his second year.
Against all horror I set such acts,
intimate and warm as gathered friends
huddled in a room against the storm
or around the table for a final meal.

Homecoming

for Tom and Catherine

I missed your wedding but caught the glow
when you returned from honeymoon, fresh
with memories crowding as you spoke — *eau
minérale*, crumbs from *baguettes*, the lush
countryside fanning from your train *en route*
to beaches of the South past market square.
I imagine you stretched on sand as the old
stare from deckchairs on long promenades.

Back here I'm afraid there's little change:
the leaking roof and faded paintwork still
annoy despite your different state.
When it poured I thought of you basking until
you seemed smooth-skinned from sun, your hair
turned slowly fair in that generous light.
Outside my window, a stifling grey,
drizzle fell to enforce the mundane.

So welcome home with your tans and rolls
of film to keep your honeymoon new. That wild
dancer you saw in a Paris street might force
his abandon upon you as the light subsides,
an image of life as it should be for you.
The showers that threaten your roof are still
not those that drive the old from strands.
Lost for shelter, they envy your clasped hands.

The Bluebell Ring

Settled in a ring of bluebells, we watch
pheasants search tall grasses for seed.
Hounds bay in kennels near the house
as if in protest at the last hunt's end.
Woods echo their cry that's tossed
amplified back to deserted yards,
the shut stables where bales are stacked.
Nothing disturbs us but a bird

clattering through trees until
its song dominates the air — a keen
whistling, sharp as a poacher's low
signal sent in warning across weirs.
We could be Lord and Lady here, or only
butler and maid. In centuries-old light
we meet near the sundial and I press
your face to mine as horses trot past.

We could plot escape, a boat to France,
servants lugging our trunks to a cove.
On avenues horses whinny and we sense
spies in the rustle of leaves and grass.
Instead we are merely ourselves, you
in a yellow dress with your hair spread
loosely over bluebells as we talk;
I eager to confide as you press my hand.

Settled in a ring of bluebells, we watch
the gardens empty as late light fades,
the spray of fountains stilled, hounds
calmed by darkness covering yards.
The last bus grumbles through the gates
and we delve into woods towards the dark.
Courtly, precise, we arrange the ground.
Your dress slips from you without a sound.

Close Comfort

Once rooms enlarged in tears and tall
neighbours crowded in comfort of strong
tea and hurried sandwiches. Uncles,
uncomfortable in black, slipped
coins to calm me, their eyes liquid.

Those eyes still surface in stress,
cliffs of loss and controlled grief
where love is a momentary foothold,
and your words, like gathering neighbours,
enclose me in their comfort.

The Smell of Cake

I love the smell of cake in kitchens,
to stand in the heat of work and feel
the air warm as baked stones.
Dough clings to wooden spoons and bowls,
the worn edges of an old recipe book.
And your hair is powdered with flour,
your palms smooth as a washed baking board.
Above all, I love the finish when, together
under the calendar that's months behind,
we swop spoons from a basin of cream and lick,
my beard flecked with it, your chin white,
and between us our son yelling for a lick,
and rising all around, the smell of rich, cooked cake.

Wedding Letter to New Delhi

for Dan and Gretta

Working at my window above the Lee now
spreading in flood across streets where rain,
poignant as some worn provincial novel,
sweeps from grey and dims the flash
of neon at the nightclub door, I think
of you in your land of caked earth and thick
heat where ponderous cattle pass: loud
laneways of Delhi where echoes hardly ring.

From here to there an infinite journey, yet
no longer than any made with pain and risk.
I imagine your wedding — an outdoor altar where
the priest in white vestments talks of home.
Around you the dense silence of the compound
where servants stare through a bamboo fence,
eyes fixing details into focus like a lens.
Or else it happens in a crumbling office, some

official flicks insects from a sill before
rapidly speaking the civic vows, his face
a dark blubber in the heat, his pen
sticky in your hand when you sign the book.
Afterwards a long meal in a friend's garden,
someone singing to a low sitar until you join
in songs with words you can hardly know.
A rustle of beaded curtains and you go.

I live in the wrong time to fill songs with pale
nymphs who surround you singing *Io! Io! Hymen Io!*
Or to talk of forests where minstrels with pipes
and tabors play to celebrate your act. I offer
what I see from my high window — the still city,
walls where shredded posters catch the rain,

doors open in flats along Wellington Road
where sports results crackle across corridors.

Does this depiction of the real depress your gay
spirits on this, your wedding day? Still, I claim
in such crude pictures lies our proper place,
that the torn paper trapped in a pool
or the squeak of an unoiled bicycle after dark
contain more wonder at the being alive
than the pined-for, chorus-haunted wood,
the conjured Orpheus with impossible lute.

With that I saw two Swannes of goodly hewe
come softly swimming downe along the Lee,
their gaze fixed on the current's flow, necks
curled against dismal showers. Around them,
cranes turn above anchored ships
and in their perfect poise I find your match:
a measured pace, oriental in its calm.
From here to Delhi let their echoes ring.

The Last Headland

i.m. Donal Foley

Ring is the place in Ireland that I really love the best.
Its fields, thatched houses, and craggy cliffs have been
with me all my life.
                            — Three Villages

In Helvick the arms of the harbour hold
trawlers and yachts from the gale's grip.
Fishermen, hands hard and frozen as ice,
haul nets to the pier, their rough curses
crude and clear as diamond against the soft
talk of those who watch behind windscreens —
tanned executives, empires expanding around
the small beaches, each hunched field.

In a pierside pub the loud jukebox drowns
the slurred voice of the last traditional
singer, head slumped against the wall
as if to recall some stray, impossible lament.
His eyes flicker shut in disappointment.
A travelling teacher of the twenties wrote
each jewelled phrase of his songs in books.
Now the clack of pool cues disturbs his daze.

Across the bay smoke from a stack gashes
the coastline. Fields of bungalows slope
towards cliffs where stone walls end,
all crumbling or bordering a manager's lawn.
Council officials jot details in the doorway
of a collapsed cottage, swift nibs enclosing
in figures what only a song could express.
Occupants await redress like a chorus.

The last thatch long ago caved in, fields
without names to tell their legends, the school
turning children towards the town and grey
factories far from the farms and harbour.
Paint peels from a signpost where hardly
a car passes, grass choking the verge.
A single bird, dark against clouds, scans
headlands where childhood dies like a language.

(1981)

The Seed of the Fire

On the day you left for America
and no one now in your own house
(though you washed the willow pattern
all the same), you carried a bucket
of fire across fields to the hearth
of a neighbour who'd keep it going
until you came back, if you ever did.

I have a picture in my mind
of the last man in the valley,
surrounded by mountains littered
with sheep and craggy rocks.
Winter and summer, his fire burns,
sending its smoke like messages to
the dot of a jet that trails a reply.

Around him the closed doors
of a dozen cottages, a few
no more than gable and sagging walls.
He hears from fewer of them at Christmas,
their large brash cards a cause
of wonder to himself and the postman,
the stamps preserved for the Missions.

His hearth is filled with their fires
and he tends their coals like lambs,
wondering when one splutters if it might
mean that someone's fading, or one
burnt to ash might mean a death.
Somewhere there's the seed of the fire,
a core of coal that contains them all.

When he goes even that will burn out,
the last fire in the valley gone
like the last word of an old language.
What can he do? In a mad dream,
he thinks of a small electric fire
plugged in forever, its bars hot
as hands that greet a cold child's face.

(1986)

Raymond Chandler in Waterford

'They were godawful snobs'
in their house on the hill with neat
hedges fixed as an old idea.
Relatives welcomed his mother back,
the American boy all talk of 'folks'.

Bored at the edge of nursery windows,
he could see a walled-in seminary
where priests in pairs walked paths,
old lecturers snoozing in oak-shade
'when a man came through the door

with a gun in his hand'. Dullness
a dust over everything, days
broken into cricket, walking, aunts,
everything hemmed-in and old.
Their snobbery was what he remembered

and, later, he blushed at being Irish
as if from something seen on the quays —
the poor, queuing at a shipping office,
a shout flung from a darkened lane.
All this was Ireland: the roots of shame.

(?1988)

Letter from Ireland

for Vincent Buckley

From sheltered Cork to the Antipodes
    I'm writing to you in troubled times,
with words like shapes on a fogged window
    made before morning shatters the mime
    of fingers on glass, chasing sublime
patterns into hiding. Before you retort,
allow me to send you this blunt report.

But why, you ask, should I pick on you
    when a million others might fit the bill?
With Patrick White and the kangaroo
    you're all I know of Australia. Still,
    ignorance can seldom daunt the will.
Why write to a poet, say, in the Golan
Heights? What would he know of Sydney Nolan?

And as you see, I've been reading Auden
    whose voice insists on fun in the house.
His reindeer haunt me night and morning
    and Brodsky loves him. I feel a louse
    saying it, but that's part of my excuse.
I'll steal a cadence like a factory siren
blaring out to you, my Australian Byron.

Things are bad here, as you surely know,
    with bombs, funerals, queues in the Exchange,
morale like mercury falling so low
    it seems about to shatter the gauge.
    While bright clothes are all the rage
our mood is of darkness gathering ground.
Pleasure's clink is a threatened sound.

I don't want to depress you in your land
    of Christmas sun and barbecues on lawns,
where the wicked prosper and, I understand,
    the good do more than think of sin and yawn
    with boredom. Brochures boast it's a dawn
for the lemming young who leave to tramp on
sand where once they tramped in Camden.

But false dawns bother me now and make
    part of why I'm writing out of the blue.
With Ireland, I feel I've bought a fake
    in a huckster's shop. It passed as true
    value at the time and accrued
worth as decades rolled while fields
gave way to factories making chalk and cheese.

They rose throughout the yielding land,
    concrete husks for profit to pour
plentiful as rainfall into soft hands
    while workers crowded to the factory floor.
    The boom is over. Now you're more
likely to find workers on the dole
and factories empty, a drained pool.

But if you read the quality press, so solemn
    in a world with no one on their uppers
but the token poor in a weekly column,
    the world's a colour spread for yuppies
    licking at fortune's bum like puppies.
The rich are gathered in thick stockades
with the poor outside, outcast as AIDS.

Is this too much first thing at morning
    in Australia brighter than gleaming gold?
I doubt if you need such a warning

since you know well what's with the old
country. Still, I feel it should be told
because since childhood I was taught I'd grow
into a dream proclaimed at the GPO.

Now the planes leave with my friends
for Boston, Sydney, Luton or Leeds.
Soon there'll be nothing on view but trends
from the past or preserved scenes,
though we'll keep regulation green
intact here where it's seldom a crime
to kill a lake with belched slime.

It's not all bad, of course, and when next
you come I'll show you places still untouched.
Walking for hours in Gougane Barra, my vexed
mind relaxes, and I feel again the lurch
of love released for sorrel, heather, birch
and pine. Walking at twilight near the lake
my mind strengthens again. In such places I take

peace like a potion: the hills grey and tinged
with heather, or studded with sheep
where cataracts flow in sunlight like thin
bangles shook under chandeliers.
But I love the streets as well, their sheer
energy. Housing estates, chip shops, machinery,
these made my childhood and remain my scenery.

My childhood landscape lacked
harvests, thatchers, blacksmith and forge.
I knew no mucky lanes and watched the backs
of houses seen from classrooms in a surge
of all I was taught not to love: my world purged

by those who said Ireland was more
real when viewed from a farmhouse door.

When I walked in fields as poets should
   I sought poetry in the rise
of hillsides and ditches, and I stood
   among cattle waiting for the bright
   truth of verses. I contrived
to turn acres into some celestial dance.
Yet none of this was my inheritance.

Instead I knew archways where at night
   we gathered among graffiti, our dull
cigarettes like cones of light
   flaring in faces as we talked of girls.
   Or I knew hedges in gardens clipped
with lost ambition, rose and privet made
to match the line of a painted gate.

This was Ireland, too. The first screens
   flickered behind curtains. I saw Lemass
cut ribbons as factories opened to meet
   workers in a promise that had come to pass.
   Latin left the Sunday Mass
and Europe beckoned until it seemed
even dogs in the road would reap the dream.

My father never walked with a plough or stood
   against walls in Boston thinking of home.
He never followed traces, or felt he should,
   since the factory opened and he learned more
   about machines making boxes. Reaper and sower
are not my images: a green button pressed
to make rollers turn was more impressive.

Where others judged by turf and swore
    faith in life out of *Ireland's Own*
I waited in bookies where my father pored
    over naps and tips. This too was Ireland, home.
    Rewards were comics or, on Fridays, cones.
Ribbons were scissored at factory gates.
Hills were bulldozed into industrial estates.

I learned off placenames like a vital code —
    the landscape of Ireland sheltered in sounds:
Mweelish, Araglen, Adrigole,
    Graigridda, Grannagh, Lombardstown.
    New suburbs changed to Blenheim Downs
while those on the up choose Chelsea Heights
or Chelmsford Village where kennels, I bet, have lights.

It was all confusion. Old worlds gave way
    to ways of looking that turned life sour
for those who wanted sepia tones to stay.
    Easter wreaths were set down
    by old rebels. Ambush sites became ground
for prayers and the boast
of freedom sealed with a hoarse Last Post.

I write from our commonwealth of art
    as Heaney called it, of *makaris flour*.
There, with trampled petals of the heart,
    I place words in ridges and tend each poor
    stray syllable. Some sounds are plants, sour
and flowerless. Others are hidden herbs
in small corners, adding zest to jaded verbs.

But still the accusation comes
    that art's an action made by boring farts
who shield their ears from pounding drums

and sit at windows where curtains part
    but quickly close when marchers pass.
I've heard it said we prefer to spout in pubs
or to scoff free dinners in university clubs.

I fear the face of the man who screams
    for poems to work like bayonets and pierce
the veins of power. Nothing I write will mean
    one jot of change in the broken streets
    of Belfast or Dublin. No words can meet
bullets and no poem I know can aid
the firm dismantling of a barricade.

If we have a duty, then it's to guard
    words like children, keep them from harm
since words create the world, and to discard
    language at its finest, to fill it with smarm
    or pushy power, is to break our last alarm.
Between *words* and *worlds* there's just an *l*
frail as the space between lovers in love's spell.

A bourgeois notion this will surely seem
    to those whose views are a stern kind
and who would ask that Homer teem
    with slaves, or analyze apartheid
    in William Faulkner. I no longer mind:
my way of looking in the end's as valid
as a barroom chorus or headstone ballad.

This, no doubt, diminishes my status
    for those who think words should pound
like artillery. They loathe the literary *comitatus*
    and claim our poets have gone to ground.
    Or else they turn the story round

and face the fifties, where the working poet
gives way to memory and the anecdote.

A nun lies dead in a televised ditch,
   a baby is bombed in a pram.
Explosions cause the slightest hitch
   as if a secret signal jammed.
   Black sacks flap near a ditched van;
drummers walk to the Republican plot,
flags dipped slightly at the sacred spot.

Black sacks on hedges, black sacks on doors,
   black plastic rustles as black hearses pass.
Refuse bags tied to telegraph poles
   signal anger at our local impasse,
   strung and stuffed, with heads to match
Thatcher or Paisley; and across a bridge some hand
has painted in white: *Remember Bobby Sands.*

Black sacks in doorways, black sacks in fields,
   black rifles uncovered on a Donegal strand.
Black border on photographs, black dresses for grief,
   black berets on coffins, black bowlers and bands,
   black bullet holes in hallways, black words of command,
black taxis, black jackets, black bruise and contusion,
black crêpe on a letterbox, the Royal Black Institution.

Death stalks the farms of South Tyrone,
   ruffles its cold clothes and changes
direction for Armagh, stopping to take home
   a soldier ambushed at greeting's range.
   Nobody seems to think it strange
when Death makes some mistake and takes
a girl as well near a farmyard gate.

No matter how I try, that theme
    slips in like fog through broken windows,
settling on everything though it seems
    beyond my reach. Again, I forgo
    my instinct for caution and let go
with rhetoric. Yet who, I ask you, could block
misery out with the blackbird over Belfast Lough?

Echoes, echoes. That old monk in his cell
    making from bird's cry a gloss
is sometimes what I'd like to be, well
    hidden by woodland, free from dross
    with nothing on my mind but women and the cross,
watercress, berries, and a fly that tells
what word I stopped at in the Book of Kells.

But life is wasted searching for the pure
    meaning of mountains or the ultimate food,
and nothing irks me more than dour
    misfortunates looking for the good
    in sandals and sea-salt, windmills and woods
where they stalk and tramp for purity, yet
still pause to roll a handmade cigarette.

I love instead mere ordinary things
    and prefer to gaze on two women talking
than on plants that grow as they sense you sing,
    while blokes communing with misty mornings
    are ditchwater-dull compared to the shrill
whistle of a train. Stuff joss sticks and ouija:
Van Morrison's worth ten of the Maharishi.

Most of what I love's more harmless and mild:
    books, chips mixed with curry, fine
typefaces, hurling, woodcuts, light

operas and spices, poker at midnight,
   the inside story of gangland fights,
chunks of Carver's prose and slow
Waldens of silence by quiet Thoreau.

In other moods I enjoy pillow talk, say,
   lightened by love, or the smell of old
shops where scales tremble with weights.
   I love deserted docklands and cold
   suburban streets where anything goes;
Mozart, I suppose, Bob Dylan if in the mood,
Ella Fitzgerald singing 'Solitude'.

My Ireland has no tin whistle wailing
   against creels and mists on open bogs.
Neither has it place for imitation
   thatch on houses, or for mock
   blather to camouflage how dog eats dog.
I have no time for the view that Ireland's
the sum of the scenes at a Munster Final.

My Ireland has no dark clichéd hag
   toothless in turfsmoke as she cackles.
I have seen the face of a woman dragged
   through bedrooms screaming, battered
   and bruised until her body blackened.
Deirdre of the Sorrows thrives
daily in the home for battered wives.

The theme is changing, my rage revives.
   Memory Ireland. They shoot heroin these
times in streets where Connolly said lives
   were lost in slumland hunger and disease
   while suburbs sat in cushioned ease.

Archaeologists talk of our early tribes
where flatlands shelter fifty thousand lives.

So you see, dear Vincent, the outlook's bad
    though still there's much to compensate.
The country's split in a thousand parts
    but old ideas still predominate.
    The peasant leaning on his gate
is now a manager pleading for more
grants while workers are shown the door.

Sometimes I go to Cobh and stare
    at water where emigrants waved
to families on the crowded pier.
    In Manhattan or Boston they saved
    enough to bring another until all were there.
Old drawings depicted a country dying:
grim men standing, shawled women crying.

The liners are pictured on walls
    in hotel lounges, generations marred
by misery and the need to pour all
    into tickets for White Star or Cunard.
    The country wears their going like a scar.
Today their relatives save to support and
send others in planes for the new diaspora.

On the coast in West Cork once I saw
    an Indian woman throw petals to the waves.
Water dripped from her sari, drenching her small
    feet as she wept into water and prayed
    for her son killed in a bombed plane.
Her words poured over the waters gathering
and receding again. She stood in shallow lather.

Often I think of her on that rough shore
    and leave her with you now as I end,
her hands filled with flowers and more
    meaning in the gesture than I can comprehend.
    Something of what she signifies I send
to you in Australia: her dignity a sign
sent out in defiance of her place and time.

(1988/89)

The Abdication

She sat in a summer house in Tipperary
in the nineteen thirties, weighed
by a gymslip and headband.
Couples chattered on a shaved lawn.
Jewels and glasses were twinkling stars
in songs her sister sang before sleep.
She spread a newspaper across pleats.

Steady as a stick in search of water,
her fingers edged along lines of print:
scandal, divorce, crisis, shock,
each word a seismic secret found out.
The world went still as cut-outs.
A globe slipped from its axis in a classroom.
The world fell loose and open like a dress.

The Word Collectors

I

They listened like informers,
gathering words to please the keen
priests and teachers,
students with hands soft as damask.

In an old book their phrases seem
speech-seeds spilling from mouths,
dust swept from a shelf collapsing
beneath rusted iron and broken tools.

Their names are rows of headstones,
a casualty list from the Somme or Dunkirk.
All that's left of them is print.
Everything about them is silence and ink.

2 IRISH

after Donal Ó Liatháin

I am a cargo ship in full sail
with no harbour in sight.
I am a book no one understands
in a language from the sky.
I am a lamp lit in a cupboard
with all the doors shut tight.

Must I stay hemmed like a ship in a bottle,
escaping like a whisper all my life?
Or will the key of Christmas flick
the lock free and let me sail
at last across the threshold?

Refugees at Cobh

We were sick of seeing the liners leave
    with our own, day in, day out, so when
the boats edged with refugees to Cobh
    it was worth the fare to travel
from Cork to glimpse them on railed decks.
    They seemed like ourselves,
their clothes were different:
    dark coats and scarves like shawls,
shoes heavy as anvils. Their talk
    thickened: accents the sound of rocks
crumbling and crunching in quarries.
    We pushed pins in the maps
of their towns and regions,
    a homeland rife with altered borders.
They hadn't a word of English but we gave
    what we could: sheets and rationed tea,
sweets, blankets, bread, bottles of stout.
    The night they sang for hours
we heard their music pour over the islands,
    and none of us recognized the words.
I still see the lights of Haulbowline
    shimmering as verses broke among waves
and then moonlight fell on silence.

    So strange to see emigrants to Ireland
huddled near posters telling us to leave
    the broken farms for New York streets.
It was our Ellis Island: hunched
    lines of foreigners with bundles
staring at the grey cathedral, the terraces
    of houses curved like icing around
hills where handkerchiefs fluttered.
    In time we turned them away. Most stood
as still as cattle when the ship drew out
    and the pilot boats trailed after it.

The Blackbird

after the Irish, 12th century

A blackbird breaks the silence
with frantic cries of grief.
His nest is torn and trampled,
the bones of his young are scattered.

Frail bird, I'll tell you this:
I know something of what you feel.
When it comes to hurt in homes
there's little for you to teach.

A lout climbed up and smashed
your home and heart in a flash.
The careful curves of your nest
are just twigs to a man like that.

Your little ones came when you called,
clustered on a steady branch.
Not one of them needs you now:
nettles thrive where you sang.

Your mate was beside you always,
her beak a bright nib of light
when that man sprung his trap
and she died, her wings sapped.

I find it hard, dear God, to live
with all that you make happen.
It sometimes seems that others thrive
while all I build lies in tatters.

Grief holds me like a shawl
weighing me down as I walk.

Nothing I say can change things.
Nothing can mend that wounded branch.

The Sheltered Nest

My sadness is a mottled bamboo.
Roots twist in torment underneath
but even before the first shoot grew
it contained a pattern of future tears.

Why bother now wipe stains from clothes?
I walk without hope by the Lee and Suir.
An old book in my hand shields me
from sunlight breaking over Inchigeela.

Bottles and bags among weeds on the Lough,
sparrows in gardens along Glasheen Road.
I watch rain speckle grey waters,
birds pass in pairs with heads bowed.

The photographs are taken from walls
leaving wallpaper lighter where they were.
I feel a new space darkening like the mark
where once a wedding ring was worn.

Day after day the gardens bloom.
Fuchsias pop open in my children's hands.
How long now before my heart's threads
float with gossamer tugged from hedges?

From Hackett's Terrace I survey quays.
No sirens sound through dead factories.
Moonlight invades a ruined playground
as I count the bridges from here to home.

When least expected I found love again,
startling as a bracelet gleaming in grass.
At odds with no one, I found ease
and shed my sadness, a stained suit.

In Gougane Barra at the end of autumn
there's little sign of the grass wilting.
I think of that crossing North Gate Bridge
and of a woman waiting, red hair unpinned.

Surf breaks with driftwood near Ballymore.
Our children skim stones on rough water.
Shadows play on a black flute
as you lean into winds filled with warning.

My tongue on your tongue is the touch
of leaf against leaf on a twisted tree.
Your breasts are fruit falling as your arms
shelter the frail nests of my cares.

Pictures from an Exhibition

for Tomáisín Ó Cíobháin

BALL UISCE

A limb of water in Connemara,
a liquid arm in a socket of peat,
glistens on a canvas and curves
like a lover's arm relaxed in sleep.

The sky is a swollen tent of rain.
Gathered storms darken clouds.
The arm stirs when brushed by winds
that skim the stretched meniscus.

THE BLASKETS

There's no one now to write down
the story of homes reduced to husks.
Who knows the folklore of a ruin
or the triad of a caved-in roof?

The last ones walk through Dunquin
as if still on the island paths —
a straight line behind each other,
a list of words for the one thing.

OLD FIELDS

The lines between them are threads
sewn to fasten the hillside down.
Old beehives in the sun, huts
bulge in corners where sheep stand.

Sheets flap between them and the road,
laundry waving in starched surrender.
If split any more, those fields will be
only stones in pockets for eldest sons.

TALK

A golden fish lurks in a well
near a strand on the road to Dingle.
To search for it is to miss it,
its cute eye dodging in the shadows.

Where a hag was cursed into stone
and a restless chieftain lingers,
one night a year there's the call
of a jilted girl at a castle window.

Grandfather's Glasses

They made him look like Gepetto
who made Pinocchio in the storybook,
his bald head bent over worked wood.
Years after he died I found them

among pension books and lighters,
flints that smelled vaguely of him.
The handles were frail threads
when I drew them apart and held

a smudged lens to the kitchen light.
I fixed them on before his mirror,
rust nicking the back of my ear;
his thin face formed in a watery blur.

Sydney Place

BEANS

What must they have grown to now,
secrets sprouting in the dark?
My arm resting on a windowsill,
I flicked mung beans at ivy
as if next morning I'd wake
to a beanstalk ripe with solutions.

THE MOBILE

It jangles in a mild breeze
above my son tucked in his cot.
Each morning he wakes and strains
to reach its impossible height,
but misses always those turning birds,
plastic fish swimming in the sky.

RAILINGS

My son swings from black railings
where once a horse was tethered.
Snow settles on his woollen hat,
crystals dissolve in strands.
In a photograph he squints ahead
to a future from which we've gone.

THE DEAD PIANIST

The pianist's funeral passes
terraces at evening, his long
fingers joined on a still stomach.

I think of John Field dead in Moscow
and hear a nocturne settling
in leaves from trees on Wellington Road.

THE BUS STATION

The passport photo booth flashes
in the bus station near the river.
I watch it from my high window:
a message sent with a mirror
from desperate souls in a valley,
frantic for answers in the far hills.

THE POET UPSTAIRS

The poet is working upstairs.
I can hear his typewriter clattering
between our arguments, poems made
among shouts and accusations:
our fierce anger a dust that clogs
the bright needle of his work.

TEA

Endless infusions, silver strainers.
teapots, bags dangling from strings
in cups where dried leaves darken.
Rosehip and hibiscus, camomile, mint,
and lapsang souchong with its smell
of woodsmoke from a forest hearth.

THE LOST WIFE

A poet by the fireside cries
for his dead wife. Whiskey draws
sadness from him like a keen.
He talks of voice, hair, skin,
holds a ring up to the light
and frames the space where she has been.

THE PARADE

A window opening on a parade,
brass pounding in McCurtain Street.
Drums reverberate and boom
the rhythm of a New Orleans funeral,
dancers behind a coffin, pearl
teeth flash against the sun.

DRIED FLOWERS

They crackle when I press them
in a vase on the grey mantelpiece,
their country colours stranded
among ashtrays and lampshades.
They are frail fossils left behind,
crisp hopes weathered and worn.

THE OLD SCHOOL

The school is gone from Belgrave Place,
rats scramble in briars near the wall.
A light burns in a closed classroom

where I sense the ghosts of children,
their pinafores pressed and the lost
future a blackboard at which they stand.

THE NIGHT SKY

A moon you could hang a coat on,
a pantomime curve in the sky.
Smog rises above roofs of the city
from homes rife with offerings
to appease it before it disappears:
the last god going in a sliver of light.

The Stone Carver

for Ken and Rachel Thompson

PRAY FOR ME, ERIC GILL, STONE CARVER 1882–1940,
AND FOR MY MOST DEAR WIFE, MARY ETHEL 1878–1961.

1

They carried your coffin in a cart
across the Chilterns. Wheels left
tracks you'd once have treasured.
You lay in straw as in a manger,

dear Mary's kiss the last on your lips
that knew so many and spoke
of Christ's genitals as a fondled form.
Old cock-of-the-walk, sex was a feast

of trussed skirts and crumpled aprons,
a quick gift gathered in stable or bed.
The papers now would call you a beast:
Sex-crazed stone man is finally dead.

2

You treated stone with a lover's tact,
edges peeled back like a thick
jumper raised as static sparkled

and you reached the last lines,
tilting the thin chisel's tip.
Dust fell like a cloud of underclothes.

3

Part of you preferred things plain,
to fashion always with strict delight,
like the breadboard you made and set
with nicked edges on a kitchen table,

crumbs scattered where tea towels
were shaken when loaves cooled
as if any moment crowds would come
ravenous from Mass on Sunday morning

and Mary's bell clang in the yard,
her hair a combed river of lines
you'd soon chisel in blocks of wood,
her apron warm and smelling of bread.

Altnasheen

Altnasheen, the gorge of the fairies, may ultimately vanish altogether as a name, for names live only as long as people have a use for them.
    — Michael Viney, *The Irish Times*

The black sewing machine rusted
among bushes at Altnasheen,
blackcurrants clustered around it
where a faded *Singer* peeled.

White sheets flapped on a line
to signal to cousins come visit,
calling cards fluttering,
handkerchiefs from a train.

I have never gone there but hear
Altnasheen unravelling on a page,
a creel of sound that I carry,
laundered linen to sort through.

I listen to its music and know
the treadle trapped by a stone.
Near it, a mouth wide in silence,
the curved horn of a gramophone.

The Pursuit of Arethusa

Jaded from chasing through woods all day
I still found time to love the way
light spilled between leaves as if poured
from a spoon tilted over the trees.
Pathways crackled with dried leaves
and twigs that snapped while birds
scattered before me like torn words.

Hair blew in my face, its curls combed out.
In pools I watched it quiver but thought
it hardly a thing to write home about.
Men whispered in its strands after feasts,
grinning with gristle between their teeth.
Not all nymphs are open like a text.
That day I yearned for water, not sex.

I wanted torrents to pour past my lips.
The forest was a stifling warmth, its heat
a clinging shawl from head to feet.
My world shrank to a need to drink
when I came to a stream and entered it.
I could count stones on its clear bed
where minnows moved in a darting script.

I looked around: not a soul; I peeled
my clothes away and sensed something turn
quieter than shadows across an urn.
Water clamped my ankles as I stood
in terror, tightening like a rinsed sheet.
I plunged when knives of sunlight cut
lines through water that broke and shook.

I heard a voice boom out my name.
Alpheus, god of the river, manic

like a dirty old man at night
watching women wash by candlelight.
I sensed his fierce desire unfurl
as I crossed my arms in panic
and ran: a panting, frightened girl.

I ran so fast my skin dried in seconds.
I could barely breathe: the world spun
in a spume of names on my tongue —
Orchomenus, Psophis, Maenalus, Erymanthus.
I blurted a list of syllables and sounds
when he rushed across the quivering ground,
his breath on my neck, his hands held out.

A child grasping a hem, I cried
to Diana, pleading that this god
dissolve in streams and pools.
A cloud formed in a sudden mist.
I entered it as if through a gate,
my limbs frozen as a roof under frost.
I was a hidden hare while hounds rage past.

He followed my steps to the last trace
where the clouds began. I knew from his face
it was all over. Sweat poured. My teeth
chattered and my skin went cold. I shook
and wished for the old safety of skirts
in kitchens where women cut meat
or yelped as I tugged at their sandals.

I edged my foot and trickles gathered.
A pool formed in the clay at my feet.
I turned to water and breached the ground
when he mingled with me and we poured

in darkness until I landed without love
in Ortygia, with a hopeless, artesian sigh.
I hid there for ages, then poured into earth above.

(Ovid, *Metamorphoses, Book V*)

Marginal Man

Thomas Merton 1915–1968

Black and white stranger in a snowy field,
your gloved hands chop wood with an axe
that cuts through bark with the flat
thud of steel through silence. A cap
heavy as a fisherman's circles your head.

Easy for me to think of you tonight
with an Irish wind howling against the glass,
a teapot cooling among sandwiches packed
for children's journeys. Shadows from plants
trail into corners where books are stashed.

Otherwise little to notice but sounds —
floorboards crackling into place and coals
collapsing in the grate. A broken tap
sounds its annoying morse while wind
whistles around bins in the wet yard.

Silence was the theme you took,
the quiet of places where nothing stirred
but pens on paper in cold scriptoria,
your knuckles cold as Gallarus or Kells.
Yet still you never let anything go:

meadowlarks singing in settled snow
moved you to scribble a margin note
while light on gables in dying fields
at times could answer your deepest need.
And while you worried about the Bomb

or agonized over a nurse you loved
a bird seen suddenly over an elm
became a koan containing everything.
The sky at evening was a parchment
flecked with lines from Japanese prints.

In Washington the meetings dragged
on and on, words snapping like sticks
as maps were altered by a mood. The Pentagon
was hardly your temple, you who loved the mat
spread loosely over the earthen floor,

who loved the simple pot and the sound
of a camera clicking as you faced the last
Shaker buildings left in cold Kentucky,
your lens aimed at a broken sash
or the peeling walls of a house that still

moved you, its message one you understood.
You were outside everything, marginal man,
forever on the edge with the necessary trash
of poems or silence, content to watch geese,
or light blazing into a teeming barn.

I keep your picture in my crowded room.
What worth your silence or your quick death,
your side scorched and the electric fan
tangled on the floor, your bare feet wet?
The monk is a bird who flies very fast.

Locusts sounding among sycamores,
light was shaken between rows of pines.
Snow fell lightly as a brushstroke
in the cold dusk when they buried you.
You who wrote of the need for peace

came home in an army plane. The teapot's cool.
The fire guts out and the house is still.
A cat cries out in a neighbour's yard
and trawlers turn towards flares at sea.
The world in the end comes down to these.

Wood-gatherer in a snowy field,
you pose on logs in rolled-up sleeves,
a Buddha at ease. Your silence spreads.
The raw gales rip yachts from moorings.
The morning's thaw is a new page turning.

'Easter Snow'

for Nuala O'Connor

When I heard that slow air first
its name held me in a warm glove.
It slipped from a flute, ascending
slowly: a bird with torn feathers.

Seamus Ennis loved it and played
over a waiting grave in Clare.
A piper in his coffin was tapped
by turned earth as the song rose.

Later, in the Naul, it was played
near another grave while Seamus lay
in his own coffin waiting,
his long fingers stiff and cold,

the song played over as if
at Easter by a graveside waiting
for the hedges to empty of all
but firm eggs tucked in snow.

Wittgenstein in Ireland

He could only think clearly in the dark
so he came to Ireland, scouring Dublin
and Wicklow for shelter where thought
might sprout in the night, a frail mushroom.

Near Arklow he wrote in a sunlit ledger.
A girl eavesdropped on pages and found
only long words, the *Schauung* and *ich*
of whatever it was he was up to.

In Connemara he found the last pool
of darkness in Europe, a clarity in rock
reached like the root of a stubborn word.
Clear as theorems, sentences formed.

On an old dictionary, his simple truth:
'The limits of my language are the limits
of my world', and around it silence —
a homeland everywhere, to make his own.

Marmalade and Mrs Mandelstam

Thank you, my dear. Marmalade, it is my childhood.
— Nadezhda Mandelstam to Bruce Chatwin

To please Nadezhda in her old age
it was useless to spout in liberal rage.
Marmalade, thrillers, the best champagne,
drew more response than relived campaigns.

Marmalade especially won her over:
a taste of life as teeming pleasure.
Its smell was girlhood, secure as shavings
curled in a schoolbag on winter evenings.

When policemen ripped her rooms apart
for poems and books they ignored the jar
that bound her to the world as much
as words transformed by poetry's touch

and drove her on when all seemed waste
but for the memory of that redemptive taste.

Eldress Bertha and the Apples

She sang for the day that was in it. The last one left, she wrote down the recipes from her Shaker world and made a book. It matched the chairs and sideboards of her sect, each recipe plain as a table. Each line was what it was and nothing more, lying on its own like the lines of a poem. She sang when her hands plunged into basins of cool flour. Husks of corn lay on a table. Watermelons, too, the pips spat out by men after work. Children ate small tomatoes whole and the juice ran down their chins. She grew cabbages and carrots, peppers and musk melons, garlic, potatoes, peas. When she made a salad she worked with the care of a quiltmaker, setting each chopped and diced thing down until a bright assembly filled the plate.

It was apples she loved most. She said their names as if they were the names of children. Talman Stuarts, she would say, they're for the summer. And Yellow Transparents, they suit the summer as well. Maiden's Blush now, that's more for the Spring. We boil Jonathans in the fall and Winesaps go well then, too. We use the Nonesuch for mincemeat pies, she would say, and Sheep's Nose and Turkey Egg apples. And for Shaker hand pies we use the Chenango or Virgin apple.

Then she sang for the day that was in it and her song stayed in the minds of those who heard it and remembered it always, as they might remember a flour stain on an old recipe book or the lingering smell of cider in a cask.

The Last Shakers

They wear round glasses and bonnets
like extras on the edge of a Western,
settled in words from Custer's time:
womenfolk, homestead, frontier.

The chairs they occupy will go
at auction when the last eldress dies,
and their houses, fresh as brochures,
will sell in nostalgia for another age.

I can warm to that spare, ascetic
achievement: order, not ornament,
in details of chairs or woven rugs,
everything finished with a grace

that makes the perfect seem natural.
They surface in *Time* or *Life*: one-page
appeasements of an unnamed instinct,
the last old women serene in porticoes.

As you sat watching a programme
where the twelve survivors spoke
(your thin-rimmed glasses like theirs),
knitting a mustard-coloured jumper,

everything about you merged with them
(even your hair bunched back with pins)
until I thought you'd suddenly shake
flour from an apron and pine for plains.

The Jewish Museum in Portobello

Ireland, they say, has the honour of being the only country
which never persecuted the jews. Do you know that? No. And
do you know why? . . .
— *Why, sir? Stephen asked, beginning to smile.*
— *Because she never let them in, Mr Deasy said solemnly.*
                                    — James Joyce, *Ulysses*

Two candles on a kitchen table,
glazed bread beneath a cloth.
You lean against cool walls
as if to dodge a searchlight.

Edelstein? Your name's Edelstein?
Exile hovers around your name —
all that's left of your lost father
fleeing from Nazis in Dortmund.

Shreds of barbed wire from a camp,
a swastika on a polished badge.
Give me instead old Mushatt the chemist,
his balms and potions to ease a graze.

We stand before unrolled scrolls,
our fingers laced like plaited loaves.
I see you pleading behind camp gates,
your hair flung among the hair of thousands.

Your father is a quiet ghost moving
in the sealed ghetto of childhood.
The souvenir mug he gave you survives,
an ark of memory you never forsake.

In Fine's shop in Terenure I buy
rye bread, chunks of kosher cheese.
Streetlights are a bright menorah
lit with singing for our feast.

Your father lacked Abraham's luck,
abandoned by angels on the Sabbath.
His loss is a closing of synagogues,
the fading of black from prayer-straps.

We kiss under a canopy of clouds,
closer than a skull-cap to its skull.
Loss is a covenant between us,
the burnt bread of your father's exile.

The Gougane Notebook

A rainbow over the lake
  cataracts on hillsides
    bright as bracelets

Trees against mountains
  a darting bird caught
    in calligraphy's fleck

After a white wedding
  confetti speckles gravel:
    paint splashed on stones

Pine trees after a storm:
  pencils strewn from a bag
    insects nudging the bark

Names of the dead in Irish
  moss on old headstones
    a fur to warm dead script

Candles in an oratory
  cool stone of a font
    rustle of reeds in water

Lovers at hotel windows
  gauze of midges
    and a moon over Allua

The silence that climbs
  these mountains with me
    lightening my luggage

Clear water over stones
  curled horns of a ram
    strands of wool in barbs

Again the falls glisten
  morse sent from hills
    signals I decipher

Ripples where a fish leaped
  its mouth a momentary O
    silent soprano

Colours changing with light
  a coat turned over and over
    canvas brushed in seconds

Snow falling on snow
  lives fluttering to earth
    settling into silence

A broken bell buried in ivy
  its tongue thick with rust
    tone turned to a thud

Stone beds where monks slept
  children hide and seek
    wind whipping with penance

A priest buried on the island
  headlights in a circle on the shore
    to light his coffin on the causeway

My place of hills and silence
  violence in faraway squares
    disruption shuffling the maps

My place of peace in crisis
  a core crumbling around me
    the mountains steady and still

A heron over the lake at evening
   its shadow on the surface
      one incomplete without the other

Flies skitter on the lake's skin
   that stillness my strength
      the waterfall's gathering roar

Doneraile Court

The Awbeg's sheet of glass snaps
and surges forward in shattered foam.
Packaged like a sonnet, the manor stands
in a frozen block of lives and stone.
Its windows mirror the landscape's curve.

A Morris Minor in the gravelled drive
snorts. Smoke sputters from its exhaust.
It is nineteen forty and Europe's skies
darken with bombers. Here, churns
clatter the coinage of creamery returns.

She walks at evening down the steps,
stilettos startle birds from trees.
She's home on holiday from the Blitz
to the worn carpets of her Irish home.
She absorbs the agony that we disown

and drives over hillsides to Farahy,
shaping a story as the car bumps
and headlights catch a fox in cones.
The world is shaped to a cancerous lung.
A wireless crackles news from Germany.

But it's nineteen ninety and I sense
her imprint on October air.
The land is tense, a stifled scream,
and I walk to ease a fresh despair.
I too could make a river weep

and trees that border my slow walk
shelter no nymphs or attentive muse.
Trout choke in streams and float
with swollen bellies towards reeds.
No woods can answer and no echoes ring.

A peacock near a sundial spreads
its feathers to make a fearsome fan.
The lawns are perfect but I walk
with a marriage lost, the papers signed.
I pocket conkers for a waiting child

as a new love forms like a sentence
carved in a tree, mutability's bole.
Lawns and poems and tales are art
arranged to shield the breaking heart.
A pigeon coos in a cracked gutter.

Nineteen forty and she stops
work to look on Ballyhoura hills.
Moths flutter near heavy curtains,
their flight a torment in the room.
Tomorrow she's off to London again.

Fifty years later I too return
to children, pages, my waiting home.
I touch red hair and my fingers burn
with ecstasy. Still no woods answer,
no echoes ring among the trees.

Workmen hammer a refurbished hall.
Smooth conveyor, the Awbeg slides past.
Nineteen ninety and I head
for home and the hard century's close,
turning in darkness where the road goes.

Throwing the Beads

A mother at Shannon, waving to her son
setting out from North Kerry, flung
a rosary beads out to the tarmac
suddenly as a lifebelt hurled from a pier.
Don't forget to say your prayers in Boston.
She saw the bright crucifix among skyscrapers,
shielding him from harm in streets out of serials,
comforting as a fat Irish cop in a gangster film
rattling his baton along a railing after dark.

Exile

1 THE BLUE EYE

after the Irish of Colmcille, 6th century

There's a sea-blue eye that stares
at Ireland drawing away.

It will never look again
at the women of Ireland, or its men.

2 THE LAST LEAVES

after the Chinese

Autumn starts at the edge of the world,
the curving edge where morning slants.
A curlew cries its tale of home
shed with blossom and the last leaves.

The Woman's Script

My dropped hairpin glistens
in the stream where he swims.
It trembles when he passes
as I lay trembling once
when he passed like a gust
across a lotus near a pool.
A heron will wear that pin
before he braids my combed hair.

Once I was a chorus girl,
then I came to Royal Wei Palace.
Carried in a carved litter,
I cracked whips as servants bowed.
I wore a peacock brooch with studs
of diamond in its beak and eyes,
but this became disappointment.
Reading old letters, I longed for Liaotung.

A bird-catcher writes and pleads
that I meet him by the river.
My husband watches as I set
my sadness down in secret script,
marks like chicken-scratches in clay.
My diary wrapped in silk is a box
to carry a body to its grave.
I am a bucket fallen in a well.

My love lives near Mount T'ai.
I long to go there but fear the road
where floods pour, avalanches fall.
I lean towards the east
as if by leaning we draw close.
What can I send him? The best jade.
The road is bad, it won't arrive.
I hide my face in a creased fan.

My love lives near Cassia Forest.
I long to go there but fear the deep
waters of river along the way.
I lean towards the south
and tears stain my stiff collar.
I gather jade plates to send him
but the road is long, they won't arrive.
I hide behind a screen of silk birds.

My love lives at Hanyang.
I long to go there but fear the high
passes among the mountains.
I lean towards the west
and tears soak my furred sleeve.
I will send him a pair of pearls.
The road is long, they won't arrive.
My heart breaks as I finger sable.

My love lives at Goose Gate Pass.
I long to go there but fear the snow
smothering the unmapped hills.
I lean towards the north.
He is a fan slipped in a sleeve.
I will send him a tray made of jade.
The road is long, it won't arrive.
I press embroidery to my face.

When I first saw him I shook
as if afraid to drop boiling water.
I longed to be a rush mat
beneath his bed, or a quilt
to guard him from winter frost.
Powdered, I wait as if he'll come.
I draw pillows close and crave
for rapture to blot out the snow.

Autumn Moon

I had never seen it so close,
the moon over Minane Bridge.
Like a Japanese poet on a path
I stood and watched as it rose
to the roar of shots and the wild

yap of hounds with a dropped bird.
Elsewhere armies stalk to war
but I open to small things —
ditches crunching with frost,
wheel-ruts in mud, the far

bark of a dog in a farmyard.
And your smooth, cool face,
the eyes dark under lids
lowered like a pietà's
against fields and moon.

Timoleague Abbey

after the Irish of Seán Ó Coileáin (?1754–1817)
'Machtnamh an Duine Dhoilíosaigh' (1813)

One night I sat sadly
as the sea's waves surged,
thinking over and over
of life's hard course.

The moon and stars were out
over tides that broke quietly.
Not a gust shook
trees or flowers.

I walked along thinking,
not noticing where I went,
when I saw the door
of a church on the path.

I stood at the door where once
the old and sick took alms
at a time when those of the house
were alive.

A twisted bench was near me.
It was made long ago
and had known clergy and even
travellers along the road.

Full of thoughts, I
sat with a hand to my face.
My tears seemed showers
falling on the grass.

I spoke my loss aloud
and wept, full of sadness.
There was a time this house
teemed with happiness,

with priests, with bells,
with hymns and books read out.
Choirs and music praised
the greatness of God.

Empty and useless ruin,
there with an ancient tower,
many's the storm that beat
and battered your walls.

Many's the rain and cold
you've been made to know
since first you were a house
for God himself.

Holy wall, grey gable,
which once adorned the land,
your destruction hurts me,
your saints scattered.

You're lonely now
without choir or psalms.
All you hear is sharp
screaming of owls.

Ivy grips your arch,
nettles cover your floor.
Foxes bark roughly above
the sound of rapids beside you.

Where larks called out
to monks singing the hours
not a tongue moves now
except for jackdaws.

Refectory without food,
dormitory without bed,
sanctuary without sacrifice
or Mass said to God.

Without abbot or rule,
without quiet brothers,
all I find is a pile
of mouldering bones.

Suppression, ignorance,
tyranny, abuse:
enemies plundered
and left you as you are.

Once I was happy too
but that was long ago.
Life turned on me.
Sorrow is my season.

My energy is sapped.
I am aimless and blind.
My friends and children
moulder in this church.

My face is grim.
My heart is a husk.
If death called now
I'd gladly welcome it.

(1989)

The Saint and the Bees

after the Martyrology of Tallaght, c.830

*A saint went walking
in Marlogue wood
amazed by light
on splayed branches.*

Woodland wove
its pine-dark spell.
He never noticed
when the Host fell.

Arm-deep in nettles,
he burrowed and dug.
Panic stumbled
in stuttered psalms.

Torrents of bees
buzzed where it lay,
fierce wings flapping:
a film wound back.

They carried the Host
away from the path,
around it formed
a tabernacle of wax.

The saint in penance
fasted for a year,
at Christmas his pleasure
wet cress by a stream.

Summer bees swarmed
(a cello slurred):
a drone from a hive,
he tumbled forward.

He came to a glen
where honey flowed.
On a limestone rock
the tabernacle stood.

Bees disappeared,
shaped wax cracked.
Among broken hives
the Host was intact.

A saint went walking
in Marlogue wood
amazed by light
on splayed branches.

(1992)

Separation

after Akhmatova

The evening path
slopes before me.
Only yesterday we were in love.
He begged me not to forget him.
Now there are only winds
and herdsmen calling,
and the clamour of cedars
by clear streams.

Three Things Pleased Him

after Akhmatova

Three things pleased him:
white peacocks, evensong,
old maps of America.
He hated children bawling,
raspberry jam with his tea,
women's hysteria —
And to think he was hitched to *me*.

To Alexander Blok

after Akhmatova

Sunday. Twelve on the dot
when I came to the poet's house.
The room large and quiet,
and the sun in the frosty air

the colour of raspberry
set over grey coils of smoke.
Soon his watchful eyes
completely took me over.

I could be lost forever
in those calm, still eyes,
yet I know the care I need
to take to avoid his gaze.

But I remember most the talk
from that smoky Sunday afternoon,
in the high house of the poet
where the Neva flows to the sea.

How Can You Look . . .

after Akhmatova

How can you look at the Neva
or stand on bridges still?
No wonder they say I grieve
since his image gripped me.
The wings of black angels cut.
I mark time to Judgement Day.
Streets blaze with fires:
bonfires of roses in snow.

The Graveyard's Dead . . .

after Akhmatova

The graveyard's dead on Sunday
where I lie under oak boards.
Come running, dearest, visit
your mother and be her guest.
Traipse hills and streams
until adults fade and disappear.
Faraway, my son's sharp eyes
will recognize the cross that's mine.
I don't expect you to know me or recall
a mother who never kissed you or rocked
you on her knee by a winter fire,
or even gave out to you,
and never once took you to Communion.

To N G Chulkova

after Akhmatova

These are the days before Spring:
the meadow at ease under piled snow,
the dry leaves rustling with pleasure,
the wind warm, tender and supple,
and the body delights in its lightness,
and you can't even tell your own house,
and the song that once drove you mad
you sing now with rapture, as if it were new.

The Muse

after Akhmatova

My life dangles by a thread at night
when I wait for her who takes no orders.
All that I cherish — glory, youth, freedom —
seems nothing before her, flute in hand.

She comes and draws back her veil.
Her eyes pierce me with attentiveness.
'Was it you,' I ask, 'who Dante heard
dictate the *Inferno*?' She answers: 'Yes.'

The Last Toast

after Akhmatova

I toast our wrecked home,
the sadness of my life.
I raise my glass to you
and the loneliness we shared,

and to mouths that betrayed us,
to cold eyes without a hint of pity,
to the brutal world and the fact
that God — even God — hasn't saved us.

Boris Pasternak

after Akhmatova

Who compared himself to a horse's eye
peers, glances, sees and knows,
and immediately puddles gleam and ice
mourns, and melts like furnace diamonds.

Drowsy backyards in a lilac haze,
country stations, logs, leaves, clouds —
a train's whistle, a watermelon's crunch,
a timid hand in a perfumed glove.

Rings, roars, grinds, breakers
crashing, and then: silence.
This means he tiptoes on pine needles
to leave unbroken the light sleep of space.

It means he counts the grains
left in shattered ears,
and that he's come again to the Daryal
Gorge from another burial, cursed and black.

And then Moscow again where feverish heat burns
and death's distant sleighbell rings.
Someone is lost two steps from his own house,
in snow up to his waist, the end imminent.

For seeing Laocoön in a wisp of smoke,
for shaping songs from cemetery thistles,
for filling earth with a fresh sound
of poems set in a discovered space,

eternal childhood is his reward,
with the vigilance and affection of the stars,
for he has inherited the earth
and shared it with every heart.

In Memory of Mikhail Bulgakov

after Akhmatova

Roses on your grave are not my gift,
nor sticks of burnt incense, but this.
You kept your magnificent air
of disdain until you died,
drank wine and cracked jokes,
the wittiest of them all
though you choked in stifling air.
You let in the awful stranger
and stayed with her alone.

Now you're dead and no one mentions
your tormented, ecstatic life.
My lone voice sounds like a flute
to mourn you at your wake.
Oh who could credit that I, half-crazy,
grieving for lost history,
smouldering on a slow fire,
who have lost and forgotten all,
would be the one to commemorate you
who were so strong, firm-willed, inventive,
and talked to me just yesterday, it seems,
hiding the pain that racked you?

Willow

after Akhmatova

Sheltered in the cool nursery
of the young century, I grew
in chequered silence. The voices
of men ignored me and I heard
instead the wind's word.
I liked burdocks and nettles
but loved the silver willow most of all.
It was my friend for years.
Its weeping branches fanned
my insomnia with dreams.
To my surprise, I outlived it.
Now, just a stump's left.
Other willows with strange voices
murmur beneath our skies
as I sit in silence, as though
a brother had died.

In 1940

after Akhmatova

I

No psalms are sung at the tomb
when an epoch is interred.
Nettles and thistles
adorn it instead.
Only gravediggers are busy,
for corpses cannot wait.
In such silence, dear God, time
can be heard going past.
Afterwards it will float
like a corpse on a river in Spring,
but no son will recognize his mother
and grandsons will turn away,
heads low in despair
as the moon swings like a pendulum.

Such a silence settles now
over stricken Paris.

2 TO LONDONERS

Time writes with impassive hand
Shakespeare's twenty-fourth play.
By the leaden river,
we, who know a bitter feast,
would rather Hamlet, Caesar, Lear,
or walk with torches as we sing
and carry Juliet, a dove, to her grave;
or peer through Macbeth's windows
as we tremble with the hired killer.
Any but this, but this, but this:
this we don't have the strength to read.

3 SHADE

What does a certain woman know about the hour of death?
— Osip Mandelstam

You were the rosiest, the best-dressed, the tallest —
why do you surface now from the broken years?
Why does memory make
your profile tremble at a carriage window?
We argued over whether you were angel or bird.
A poet called you the Straw.
Tender light fell on us all
through the dark lashes of your Georgian eyes.
Dear Shade, forgive me — clear weather, Flaubert,
insomnia, lilacs in late flower,
all turned my thoughts towards you,
Beauty of 1913,
and your languid, cloudless day —
O Shade, these memories trouble me now.

4

I was certain that I knew
each path and pit of insomnia
but this is a cavalry charge
made to a blast of trumpets.
I enter empty houses
which once were someone's home.
Everything is quiet but for shadows
floating in a stranger's mirrors
and there, in the mist, what forms?
Denmark? Norway? Or have I lived
here before and is this
a new printing of moments forever lost?

5

I warn you
that I am alive for the last time.
Not as a swallow or maple,
not as a reed or star,
not as spring water
or bells ringing
will I come back to torment you
or to walk in other's dreams
with moans impossible to console.

Cleopatra

after Akhmatova

I am air and fire . . .
                    — Shakespeare

Already, she has kissed dead Antony's lips
and wept before Augustus on her knees.
Her servants have betrayed her. Night slips
in as Roman trumpets blare beneath eagles.

The last her loveliness taunts comes in,
swarthy and tall with a blatant whisper:
'Let you walk before him like a slave in triumph.'
The swan's slope of her neck stays still.

Tomorrow, her children in chains. O hardly
anything's left to do but tease this fool
and, like a last act of pity, set
the black snake indifferently on her dark breast.

Tashkent in Bloom

after Akhmatova

1

As if taking orders,
Tashkent suddenly lit up —
brightness in every courtyard,
a white apparition of light.
Their breath was easier than words to grasp
but their reflection was doomed to lie
in ditches under blazing skies.

2

I will remember the starry roof
in a radiance of endless praise,
and youngsters in the arms
of dark-haired mothers.

Requiem

I stood among my own,
not under foreign skies
or sheltered by foreign wings,
and I survived that time, that place.

❖

Over a period of seventeen months during the Yezhov terror
I queued outside the prison in Leningrad. One day someone
in the crowd seemed to pinpoint me. A woman whose lips
were blue with the cold was standing behind me. She knew
nothing about me but she snapped out of that trance in which
we all stood. People spoke only in whispers then, and she
whispered too: 'Can you describe this?' she asked.
     'Yes,' I said, 'I can.'
     And what looked like the trace of a smile passed across what
had once been her face.

❖

DEDICATION

This sadness makes the mountains bend.
It stops the river where it flows.
Yet it cannot break the bolts that bar
our prisoners from us where we wait.
Some feel fresh winds that blow,
some know the night from day,
some sense the sunlight as it falls,
but we hear only a soldier's boots
and the twist of keys in a cell's lock.
We rise early as if for first Mass
and walk through streets past the Neva
in mist, and the sun that barely stirs.
Hope was always a faraway song.

Whose sentence was it this time?
A cry, then her tears flowed
to single her out from the others.
It's as if her heart's been torn out
as she sways, then walks away.
I was in hell for those two years
with those friends I remember now.
What haunts them now in frost beyond
the moon's circle? I cry
out to them all: So long, goodbye.

❖

PROLOGUE

Only the dead smiled then,
glad to be out of their misery.
Leningrad was a sign that swayed
uselessly outside the prison.
The railway yards teemed
with crowds condemned to go.
Contempt was the train-whistle's song.
The stars of death shone over us.
Innocent Russia squirmed
beneath bloodstained boots
and the wheels of Black Marias.

I

They took you away at dawn.
Barely awake, I followed
like a mourner behind a corpse.
Children cried in a dark room.
A blessed candle spurted for air.

Your lips were cold where they kissed
an ikon. Sweat broke on your brow.
I will cry out to the stones.
I will weep at the Kremlin walls.

    2

Gently moves the gentle Don.
Moonlight on a windowsill stops

when it sees a shade stir —
a woman sick to the bone

lying there alone.
Husband dead. Son jailed.

Pray for me.
Pray.

    3

It certainly isn't me.
It must be someone else for I
could never bear such suffering.
Take this thing and bury it.
Take away the lamps
and leave the night.

    4

You should have been told, you old
rogue and chancer, a slip of a girl

with your gamey eye and careful charm,
you should have been told of this end:
Number 300 in a long
queue with your parcel, as tears
scorch the ice on New Year's Eve
where the prison poplar bends.
Not a single sound can be heard
though so many lives now end.

5

I have called you back and cried
for seventeen months, my lost son
changed from a man to a nightmare.
I've licked the hangman's boots.
Chaos is my element and I
no longer know who's man or beast
or even when the rope will tighten.
I know nothing only flowers in dust,
the sound of shaken censers, tracks
that trail and dribble nowhere.
The night is a stone where a star
looks me straight in the eye.
That star is the death I wish for soon.

6

The weeks fly past in a twinkle.
I can't grasp it: how white
nights slip into my son's prison
and fall again now with eyes
fixed on the Cross where you hang;
they watch for death.

7 THE SENTENCE

The word was a stone that fell
on my breast that's heaving still.
It was no surprise when spoken
and I'll get by, whatever the case.

I'm up to my eyes in things to do:
anything that kills memory and pain,
anything that makes my heart a stone
and still explains how to live again.

Summer will traipse in and insist
on dancing and sun despite my mood.
I knew this a long time ago:
a brilliant day and a deserted house.

8 TO DEATH

You might as well come now if at all.
The lights are off and the door's open.
Take any shape you like: pierce me
like a pellet or choke me like a strangler.
Infect me with typhus or spring from old
fairytales you've formed for telling on stairs
when a pale janitor leads policemen to rooms.
It's all the one to me. The Yenisey swirls.
The North Star glistens. Those eyes I love
are closing now on this last horror.

9

Already the wings of madness
trail across my mind.
It's like a wine I drink,
dark valley that draws me.

I'm a beaten dog.
Madness wins. No time
for anything now but the wild
ramblings of a stranger.

No use even to fall
on my knees for mercy.
I own nothing and now
I have nothing left to take,

not the stone face of sadness,
not my son's eyes cut in grief,
not the storm or its day,
not even the trauma of visiting hour

or his dear, cool hands
or, dimmed by distance,
the shade of lime trees,
or his last consoling words.

10 CRUCIFIXION

Choirs of angels exalted the hour.
Heaven was shattered by fire.
'Father, why hast thou forsaken me?
Mother, do not weep for me.'

Tormented Magdalene watched and wept.
A disciple went still as stone.
His mother watched quietly. They took
notice of her there, but none dared look.

❖

EPILOGUE

I

I learned how faces can fall apart,
how eyelids hide the shadow of fear,
how hurt cuts into a cheek
the runes and hieroglyphs of pain;
how blonde and black hair turns silver
and how smiles leave compliant mouths;
how fear can be caught in a cough.
    I pray now for others besides myself.
    I pray for those who stood in cold
    queues or in summer's warmth
    near the red walls of that jail.

2

The anniversary's near again.
I can reach out and see and touch

you all: you we carried all the way
to the head of the queue, and who are dead.

Or you, the girl with beautiful hair
who says: 'This is like a homecoming.'

I want to name you all one by one
but can't because the list is lost.

I have sewn a shroud from words,
threaded with sounds they whispered.

I promise to always remember them.
And if they manage to gag my mouth

through which a million cry out,
then let me be remembered as well.

And if ever this country demands
a monument erected to my name

I agree, but stipulate:
not by the sea near where I was born

for my links with waves are broken.
And neither set it in a palace garden

near a stump where shadows search me out
but here, where for three hundred hours

I stood and waited before these doors
which never once opened to let me in.

Even in the peace of death I'm afraid
to forget the scream of Black Marias

or the whinge of that terrible gate
or the old woman howling like an animal.

From my bronze eyes may snow
trickle down like teardrops

and may prison birds coo above me
as ships sail slowly down the Neva.

Could Beatrice Write . . .

after Akhmatova

Could Beatrice write with Dante's power
or Laura glorify love's pain?
I paved a path for women poets.
Dear God, how can I shut them up again?

Two

after Akhmatova

THE DEATH OF SOPHOCLES

That night an eagle flew down
to land on Sophocles' house.
Cicadas clamoured in the garden
as genius headed to immortality,
skirting the enemy fires
that glowed outside the city walls.
Then the king had a strange dream:
Dionysus told him to lift the siege
and let no sound sully the ceremony
or mar Athenian elegies for his shade.

ALEXANDER AT THEBES

The young king was parched of pity
when he told his general to wipe out Thebes.
The old officer stared at the city, memory
moved by the thought of its former pride.

Raze it to the ground! The king listed
the city's wonders — temple, tower and gate,
until he suddenly blazed with an idea:
'Make sure the house of the poet is spared.'

There are Four of Us

after Akhmatova

I renounce all that I own
and rid myself of all my things.
The guardian of this place is a worn
tree stump stranded in water.

Earth briefly takes us as guests
whose lives are habits we must break.
On paths of air I think I hear
two friends' voices, talking in turn.

Was it two, I said? There, by the east
wall where brambles twist and trail —
look, it's a dark elderberry branch,
surely a letter from Marina!

Lullaby

after Akhmatova

I bend over the cradle
like a black fir.
   Lullay, lullay.

No sign of a falcon
far or near.
   Lullay, lullay,
   my little one.

       26 August 1949
        (afternoon)
      Fountain House

A Memory

after Sorley Maclean

I remember nothing of that day,
nothing of what you said or wore,
except the smell of crushed mint
and the rush of waters at Bohernabreena.

(?1988)

The Frail Sprig

for Idit

The night is freezing hard. Frost
stiffens grass where I walk and watch
a full moon rising over our small, lost
planet no saviour now can touch.

You pose in blue in a photograph
set near my table and its waiting reams.
The dark floss of your hair enfolds
a face where smiles and hurt combine.

You look like one who knows the worth
of holding on or letting go.
Aglish, Roanmore, Dunhill, Gaultier,
I set my names against those you know:

Tiberias, Sinai, Beersheva, 'Amir.
When you were playing among the screams
of a six-day war, and begging to sleep
in bomb shelters as if dreams

might filter through trembling ground,
I burrowed in books in provincial streets.
Now, I trample hurt: a mound
where you lie waiting as I need

to leave pain behind, the used
chrysalis that yields a butterfly.
You haunt my movement like a muse.
Tonight I read Neruda, a wish unfurled:

'I want to do with you what Spring
does with the cherry blossom' — a dream
from our shared Japan and its snow
over leaves afloat on streams

where water is smooth as a kimono.
Against the night that's set in cold,
I place this frail sprig like a bowl
before a shrine. May it last and grow.

(1995)

Healing Oil

It stays on my skin for hours —
sandalwood and orange: balm
over shoulders as over wounds.

I want to hold that scent
like air in the lungs of a singer
reaching a high note in a hall

swollen with tension as if soon
the note might splinter and crack.
Instead, it lasts and leaves

a skin of silence until applause
erupts around it, and I
succumb to the memory of your kind hands.

(1995)

Lettercollum Love Song

We turn back fresh sheets
and settle bunched pillows.
You lower the lamp to the floor
as the room fills with oil-scent.

Your body is a prayer mat,
our touch delicate as lute strings.
In the long valley of solitude
I travel within you and explore

as if I prise an oyster open
to reach the perfect pearl,
or plunge like a high sail dipping
between waves in a frantic sea.

White cups on a silver tray,
mint tea cooling in a pot.
Our mouths meet like mirrors
facing across a room.

Light invades as morning comes.
Through the curtain I watch
dawn break on a ploughed field
and mistake it for a rippling sea.

Afterwards we walk in walled gardens
among parsley beds and potato drills.
Rain on young shoots falls
lightly as a blessing when we kiss.

(1995)

After the Welsh

A man past forty
may flourish like a tree
but a grave opened
changes his face.

Letter to Lisbon

All night I was alone.
I heard only the sound
of a convent bell at dawn,
the syllables of your name
in each peal and its aftermath.

❖

I float on the river
of what happens:
a boat adrift
when the rudder's lost.
You are with me. River banks beckon.

❖

To touch your sleeve now
would just be enough.
Even that would be better
than the long night ahead
knowing you will not call.

❖

If I were a leaf loosened
from a tree near your room
I would float to your sill
and wait for you to take me
to mark the last page you read.

❖

I have given up doubt,
that old, worn-out coat.
All that's constant
is the fact of change:
pearl of love, grit of pain.

❖

My room warms my work:
the deep fire reddening.
Yet nothing touches me
like the heat of your hand
against my closed eyelids.

❖

One day you linked arms
and my arm tingles still
as if even through winter coats
touch traces the line
that led us to each other.

❖

Moorhens close their wings.
Cats curl near the fireguard.
My children huddle and sigh.
With the fact of your absence,
am I the only one awake in the world?

❖

I think of you asleep.
I want to reach across Europe
to trace your hair and stroke
your face as I would a child's,
your breath warm wool on my fingers.

❖

Once I flicked a crumb
from your skirt in a restaurant.
What lies I make my hands tell:
what could I care for crumbs?
It was you I wanted to touch.

❖

In wild moments I wonder
would I be better as a bullfrog
from some Japanese poem,
wet and croaking at your feet,
offering my song like a handsel?

❖

Light which has no feeling
can reach you through a chink.
Mirrors can hold your face;
dead walls know your touch.
Yet I who want you must do without.

❖

I look at the hand you held.
It flops and seems inert
(so plain with long fingers,
the nails I barely bite),
but for the memory of your hand.

❖

Cold rooms of your girlhood,
dull lanes of Macclesfield.
Closed streets of my boyhood,
coums and lakes of Waterford.
As if at the Equator, they meet in our talk.

❖

I hear a blackbird's call
in the mist each morning.
I say your name as if sound
might stretch across space
like the bird's clear song.

❖

Your shells line a sill.
I hold one to my ear
and hear the sea heaving,
its slow, repetitive rhythm
a lesson in patience I must learn.

❖

I walk on a cliff and count
the lights of fishing boats:
fireflies on a dark sea.
Such lights are our days together.
Around them, absence darkens.

Wishing for the Border

I want to sit with you in a warm kitchen.
Outside it is raining. Steam rises

from our clothes on the silver bar
of the range where a kettle heats.

On the table a knife, chunks
of bread baked this morning.

You go to your room and change.
Through the door, I hear that song —

the one you sang an hour ago
before we kissed on a road in rain

lit by the glare of cars
panning us: searchlights in a camp.

I eat and watch you comb red hair,
your head aslant before a mirror.

Now let us lie closer than refugees,
our lips touching in the attic dark

while around us the landscape is still
as a held breath, the only sound

a dog barking across fields —
a farmyard animal, or a border guard's.

Still Lives

Shells and dried flowers,
a row of antique bottles
(phials from a closed pharmacy,
powder hardened on glass),
and light through a skylight
in annunciation.

❖

The still life of your corner —
a half-read book, stray
strands of hair in a brush,
ampoules of soap and a torn
envelope near a nightdress:
all of it framed with your presence.

❖

Torch songs in an empty room.
With you gone, who can I tell
of that slow descending note
or that phrase where a voice cracks
and quivers with heartbreak?
I save it like news for your return.

❖

The scraps of a life together —
tree houses in a child's drawing,
crumbs on a chipped breadboard,
herbs bundled near a cookbook,
autumn stripping a sapling's leaves —
I never notice when you are here.

❖

Your smell stays in the sheets.
I lie on your side of the bed
and inhale our last lovemaking,
the memory opening like a cave
towards which I swell and surge
as your lost cries mingle with bells.

❖

I wake in the night and turn
to the cold that takes your place.
Above our skylight the stars
make shapes that shine on you
in a far country. Among them, the moon
grants us equal light.

One Sunday in the Gearagh

In the long grass of the Gearagh
   you stretch and sleep
     your head at an angle to my head

A moth flits
   and hovers above you
     makes a light brooch in your hair

Cows mooch in damp fields
   lazy heads lifted
     when we pass on thin paths

Stumps of trees around us
   a drowned forest and a drowned
     village called Annahala

Lichen on trees, moss on stones,
   sparrows — nifty commas —
     dart on the sky's wide page

I tell you of the man who rowed
   across the waters to his house
     and drowned on his way home

Afternoon of perfume
   flowers crushed beneath feet
     scents yielded like secrets

Bog cotton in a meadow
   lighter than your hair
     your fingers lighter than leaves

Your face smooth against mine
   a slim wind between us
     the ghost of an old argument

Scanning the lake for otters
   we settle for paired swans
      white porcelain among reeds

Islands stud the waters
   legions of the drowned
      raising their torn heads

Meadows shimmer with movement
   tortoiseshell and meadow-brown
      butterflies in a haze of heat

I stroke your closed eyes
   and kiss the lids. I nudge
      the tip of each light lash

Oak stumps everywhere
   suppurating wounds
      the black days we have known

A heron stands
   sentry over water
      curled initial on vellum

As we cross old quarry roads
   hands linked like branches
      of rose trees in a ballad

Three Love Poems

after Paul Éluard

THE WOMAN IN LOVE

She stands on my eyelids
and her hair is in mine.
She has my hands' shape
and the colour of my eyes.
She is swallowed in my shadow
like a stone beneath the sky.

Her eyes forever open
and she will not let me sleep.
Her dreams make suns evaporate
in the broad light of day,
make me laugh, cry and laugh,
even when there's nothing to say.

NO ONE CAN KNOW ME

No one can know me better
than you have known me

Your eyes in which we sleep
both together
make for my man's glare
a fate better than any made for the world's night

Your eyes in which I voyage
give to road signs a meaning
detached from the earth

In your eyes all those who reveal
our infinite solitude
are no longer what they thought

No one can know you
better than I know you

AT THE WINDOW

My brow against the panes
nightwatchmen of sorrow
sky with darkness I surpass
plains tiny in my open hands
inert indifferent

My brow against the panes
nightwatchmen of sorrow
I seek you without hope
way beyond myself
and I love you so much
I can no longer tell which of us is absent.

The Butterfly Soul

Butterflies freed
from nets at a wine-party
circle and fly

to the fairest
there, landing on hair
with poised wings:

spirits of emperors,
souls of ancestors, lost
lovers in a daze.

As if in a world
without enmity, they trust
tanks, guns, glint

of a bayonet's edge,
or a soldier's corpse,
his spirit fled

and fluttering
on a finger at the Somme,
trembling at a nail.

A fallen flower
searching for a branch, it
floats in silence.

A man dreamed
he was a butterfly, then woke
in a wingless world

wishing for flight
to a bamboo room, keeping
a promise in love

like the butterfly
landing on a hairpin to choose
an emperor's wife

or another who flew
to a cemetery set with flowers,
wings cracked with grief.

On the edge of lush
cabbages one flutters, set
like a brooch on a coat —

a soul in flight
above my writing table,
perched on the edge

of my paper space,
an ancestor's visit
landing in a furious

flutter near my hand:
silent applause or reproof
for powdered palms.

As a child I killed
one, its death in the garden
a catastrophe of wings,

broken sails adrift,
its body ripped, while I waited
wishing for flight

to absolve the act
learning that cruelty, pain
wait in a chrysalis,

then hover and alight
on lives, our wings too frail
against such weather.

The Art of Tea

LEAVES

Let them be creased
like a horseman's boot,
curled like the dewlap
of a bullock.
Let them unfold
like mist in a ravine,
turn wet and soft
like earth rinsed with rain.

CUP

The blue glaze
of southern jade:
the perfect hollow
of a teacup.

Stir with
a bamboo whisk.
Drink and feel
the soul flood.

BOILING

Bubbles begin:
the eyes of fishes.
Bubbles swell:
crystals in a pool.
Bubbles burst:
waves in a storm.

TEA ROOM

Let it be solitary
as a cottage on a beach.
Let no sword sully
this abode of vacancy.
With linen napkin
and bamboo dipper,
let it be a shrine
for the ordinary,
for talk of tea
and the taking of tea,
best made with water
from a mountain spring.

A Shrine for Lafcadio Hearn, 1850–1904

Like an artist painting on rice grains,
he tried to trap Japan in a story:
his one good eye so close to the page
he might have been a jeweller with a gem.

So much to tell: kimonos and cranes,
cemeteries to stalk at evening, slow
shoals of candles — souls
on rivers beneath a massive moon.

Even the sound of sandals on a bridge
stayed in the mind for an evening,
matching the shadow of fishermen
on still waters: a painted print.

Or a face smiling to hide its grief,
the touch of passing sleeves
part of a plan that maps the future,
a heron seeking the heights on a wall.

Loneliness ended in Matsue: that raw
pain no longer gnawing like the Creole
songs on a sidewalk in New Orleans.
Instead he heard a flute's clear note.

He was a lantern drifting from the shore,
dissolving in the tone of a struck bell.
Sipping green tea in Tokyo, he heard
ghost stories from an impossible past

and died past fifty from his Western heart.
Afterwards, he was a story still told, set
firmly as rocks in a Zen garden.
Incense burns near cake at his shrine.

In the sound of sandals on a bridge
I hear him sometimes, or catch him
in the swift calligraphy of a scroll,
or in the curve of a rough bowl.

A breeze through a bamboo grove,
his memory passes for an instant.
Snow falls on his grave and on plum blossom.
He is fading like a fisherman in mist.

Shiatsu Sequence

SHOES

As if before a temple,
I leave my shoes outside:
clutter in a corner,
cares that I discard.

THE MAT

I press my face against it,
its smell of herbs and oil:
a pattern rich with potions,
stories it's absorbed.

CHIMES

Cylinders wait for the wind
to claim their metal song.
Watching them, I wait for you
to free hurt like a bird.

KNOTS

Muscles ease at your touch,
nets of knots you discover.
You work until they open:
a mother loosening laces.

TEARS

Tears pour as if a prophet
tapped a rock with a stick.
You draw them out: threads
to twist in comfort's rug.

OIL

Its smell fills the room,
a rattle of jars and bowls.
The sound of it pouring:
milk from tiny teats.

SCARF

A heron flashes from reeds
and grips the fish in a pool.
It is over: your peace a scarf
in which my cares lie bundled.

Matching the Note

A piano tinkles as a cradle rocks,
a lullaby tapped in tuned morse
when a blackbird stops at a window,
adding to the song its own sound.
It pecks at berries and then,
as if to match the ivory note,
resumes its music on the sill
in a world where wishes seem granted.

Russians in Paris

1

When cities crumbled before the Reds
and houses were broken by hordes
(double bedrooms now to sleep twelve,
library shelves axed for firewood),
they slid across Europe in trains,
huddled in fur, with the soft
faces of frightened animals.
History was a hopeless arrogance
where postmen became commissars,
the summer house an office
where former serfs ruled
over a future blacker than caviar.

2

In Paris life went on and breath
seldom froze in the winter air.
Children rolled hoops on lawns
and wives shopped on boulevards
that, at a stretch, matched Moscow.
At home with chants of bearded priests,
incense rose before ikons smuggled
with roubles, silver, a loved toy.
The Seine was no Volga but still
it beat the bottom of a stream
or a grave in gardens where once
the seasons seemed made by moods.
Their sleeping daughters looked
lost daughters of the murdered tsar.

3

The shop on the Mont Ste-Geneviève
is a gloomy dacha on the hill's slope.
Among ikons and toys, stacks
of books and pictures of patriarchs,
I saw two posters of poets on a wall.
One died in a camp, his poems kept
by a wife who absorbed them like food.
Another knew how poems could draw
Black Marias at the heart of night.
I know her poems like prayers,
their words clustered berries
on a branch to which I hold.
When I ask the poster's price
I am told: *She is not for sale.*

4

Violins on steps of the church,
petals over furred heads.
Funeral of the film maker,
funeral of the dancer whose eyes
loomed from Calvary at the end.
Flowers teem in a cemetery
bright with resurrection.
The dancer was a wounded faun,
a face full of age and answers.
His coffin moved through Paris
like music through the memory
as all of them move now
across steppes of time in snow.

The Lesson

Toy boats in the Luxembourg Gardens
circle small oceans to the roar
of children engrossed in the lesson
of life as an abandoned shore.

Heading for Crete

i.m. Claire Barker

Did you ever think you'd see the day
I'd write a poem with your name
and *in memoriam* at the head of it?

When I called to you in hospital
your skin was a worn parchment,
worry lines quilled around your eyes

as you curled to meet the pain's demand.
My every word came out so bland
while you, withered in a white

cardigan, a drip fang in your wrist,
watched a mirror and palmed into place
your hair that thinned with therapy.

Your room was a storm of flowers in bowls.
You slipped in and out of sleep's lair,
fingers searching for water or a comb.

Claire, you had more pillows than the princess
in the tale had mattresses over the pea,
and still you too felt the hard pain start.

You said when this was over you were going
to Crete, to bask among islands and ruined
palaces in the Mediterranean sun.

Beside you, fruit was piled in bowls
with wholefood bars, nuts and grapes,
as if by taking all that's perfect

you could blunt the pincer's edge.
Before leaving I kissed you and your lips
were powdery moth wings. Years on,

I think of that touch and of you in Crete,
the sea glinting like a raised axe
and your arm waving as the tide turns.

A *Leaf in* The Aeneid

for Ellen Beardsley

In your copy of *The Aeneid*, there's
a leaf pressed between pages.
Its stem stiff and dry, it marks

the wooden horse of Troy, a belly
heavy with death in a Greek gift.
Veins twist through the leaf like tales

spun around a winter fire.
It lasts with language handed down
as I hand this gift to you who love

and have learned to trust horses,
who found in firm mane and swivelling eye
trust without treachery, no hiding hurt.

Five Photographs by Thomas Merton

The observed particulars take on the mystery of revelation . . .

THE HERMITAGE

A house for quiet built in the woods,
one good place for a man alone.
Trees surround it and jets fly over
halfway through a psalm, words caught
in the slipstream and blown away.
It sits within the lens and seems
a shack for solitude in the wide world.

STILL LIFE

A chair, a ladder, a bowl, wood
strewn with shavings on a plain floor.
Behind the chair, an old cup stained
with rainwater. Singled within
the frame he fixed, they are firm
and plain, mundane as the shadow
of chair on bowl, ladder-rung on chair.

THE BROOM

The broom in a corner remains
no more than a broom, its bristles
firm when fingers press,
its handle smooth from months of use.
There are no messages here; no moral lurks
in the plain wall or the bunched broom.
Take it or leave it. It swishes and sweeps.

IKONS

From a distance, they might be framed
pictures of high-school friendships,
students with scrolls and gowns,
family portraits in studios.
Closer, a worn madonna pines
on painted wood. Near her, the flecked
faces of prophets stare.

WRITING TABLE

Words spilt despite the silence,
a curved lamp over them as they formed
in spiral notebooks. So little
to say for it: its sheaves of paper,
its marked book and pair of pens.
All it lacks is a mouse from Kells,
perched on a word while the monk sleeps.

Simone Weil, 1909–1943

A mind enclosed in language is in prison . . .

I have come to love you in photographs,
your thin face never yielding to ease
and your coat about you like a cape
gathered against the cold of quaysides.
I passed your old school near the Pantheon
and imagined you among children walking
near pillars pocked with bullet-holes.

You would have spent your life before
Leonardo's *Last Supper*, lured by lines
that draw you always to Christ's face.
You limped around Italy in the peace
of paintings and darkened chapels
but I think of you most in France,
an abbey at evening as chant soars

and settles in a shawl of silence.
You spread books across the floor
and peered as if words were ants
teeming on the page as in a crack
where meaning, like light, might fall.
When you died starving, waiting on God,
no realm of words could call you back.

Sisters

MARTHA

Her mind a packed picnic basket,
a woman so busy she calls
boys by brothers' names and longs
for hours alone in olive groves.
Her dreamy sister hunkers near the low-
voiced visitor whose talk she'd follow
if goats were gathered and basil plucked.

MARY

To sit in silence and listen
as pots chortle and oil in urns
warms near a sunlit doorway —
an act more simple than frisking
crumbs from aprons, or arching
a fine finger in trails of dust —
and yet like this to enter history.

The Petition

Grey Gobnait stands above a lone
woman kneeling in grass near a well.
Cattle slouch over acres
carrying their own weight like weights
of the world on the woman's mind.
She tightens her scarf and prays.

Cold water from the well,
the plastic cup cracked and peeling.
Like a cloak on the saint's shoulders
quiet settles on the evening.
On a heavy stick, the woman walks
towards Ballyvourney and Ballymakeera.

The Egg Collector

In a dark corner of the rectory, he placed eggs in rows in a mahogany case. Some were slightly cracked as if taken while swollen with birth. He thought of the firm life inside, unhatched and hopeless: a song stopped in a throat. His daughter painted watercolours in another room and, by the fire in the drawing-room, his wife worked at silhouettes. He consulted his egg books, loving the clear plates of the Reverend Morris. Each egg seemed suspended in space: a plain or speckled planet floating in the clear sky of the page. The thought of Mr Darwin darted through his mind but he banished it like a cobweb. Golden Eagle. Crow. Black-headed Bunting. Chaffinch. Sedge Warbler. Lesser Whitethroat. Specimens sent from Oxford rooms. Tomorrow, a parcel would arrive bearing, packed in straw, the egg of the Grey Plover, sent by the Reverend Tristram in Durham. He trembled at the thought, holding the pale egg of a Kingfisher in his hands as if his palms that earlier rested on the wide pages of a Bible had now become interlaced nests.

From his window, he saw moonlight fall on headstones: so many he had seen buried, his black stole flapping in the breeze over delicate girls and bearded patriarchs. He held an egg high and surveyed the sky behind it, the shell a focus for all that was frail. His daughter's laughter reached him. He closed the lid on the case and imagined the chirps of birds pleading to be released. He shoved the thought aside. So much was hardly worth thinking about. Others could make the century tremble and crack and roll. Tomorrow his parcel will arrive and his hands will part the rustling straw.

Three Women in January

A January evening of imminent snow.
I pace my garden and search
gaps in hedges as if to know
some space where answers fall to earth.
Clothes in the machine spin round
and smog smothers the stars that fail
to pierce the city's weight of soot.
Taut grass crunches beneath my boots.

The night reminds of an absent friend,
asleep near a fallen book or now
awake to soothe a restless child
who'll wake to whistle with birds.
Her cottage faces a road of ghosts.
In the garden a swing is still.
Near her, a plant stirs on a sill
as if sensing a snowflake's fall.

The scent of crushed rosemary brings
another to mind as the first flakes float,
her dark hair curled and her hands
deft as a lacemaker's when she draws
patterns in space to declare a point.
Things that summon her I can quote —
gusts that graze like an angel's wing,
the wooden button of a duffel coat.

In my slanted attic another sleeps
whose touch I sense, whose trust I keep.
Snow falls fast and blurs the fine
cloth of her blouse on the stiff line.
Buds thicken on the tree she planted,
its bare branches no more than strokes.
The curve she makes when fast asleep
I'll curl towards later, a shape complete.

Light from windows frames the edged
tracery of hedges frosted with webs.
Drops freeze and dangle from threads.
The machine goes still, a sudden death.
Cats cry out among the yards
and moonlight breaks the wall of smog,
that sight a blessing now that spills
on women, friendship, the filled hedges.

Francis Ledwidge's Cottage

I remember his small poems, country
intimacies in fading ink;
an old fiddle, books, a small
Virgin set in a shell from the Front.
In the garden, bees seemed from a page.

It became the measure of what followed,
a day of devoured happiness,
our breaths in the dark of tumuli
crossing in a single cloud.
Nothing again could ever live up to it.

In a photograph we stand at the door,
your hair in the wind, my beard that's shaved.
We could be some couple looking for roots
at the homestead where it all began,
heady with achievement of a moment's grace.

Time and the Island

for Diarmuid Ó Drisceoil

THE PACT

When she left the island and married
into Schull, she made her husband swear
to bury her on Cape when the time came.
When she died, boats carried
her corpse beneath cliffs and sailed
in the shape of a cross on the open sea
with her bright coffin at its core,
and her husband near it to guide her home.

ASHES

In the weeks before he died, the old
storyteller whose talk became books
ripped pages, rooted out poems
from cupboards, boxes, dressers and tins.
He burned them in a barrel out the back
as cancer gathered inside him and wore
away all that saw worth in words.
Ashes flecked his face as the blaze roared.

LOUGH IORAL

Near the lake with magic waters I walk
over washerwomen's flat stones. As if
for a stiff-collared photographer, ghosts
pose as petticoats are stretched
and slapped with a fury that blends
with cross-talk in a sepia morning.

I move among them and their words
that time tore: threads from a hem.

WALLS

Sunlight spills between grey
walls that snake through fields.
A stone shifts from a place it kept
for centuries and disturbs
the rhythm of a wall that shivers slightly.
Windmills wave their frantic arms.
Coves cry against the push of breakers.
Tokens of lost time, small flowers break through.

THE OLD CHURCH

Sheltering from rain in the saint's church,
I trace the line of lintel and sill.
Through thin windows, sermons distil
meanings that make the moment change.
Headstones lean in the grass where wet
scythes curve until the downpour stops.
Behind me, a generator hums with the drone
of monks at compline on a winter evening.

CAR DOOR

A car door blocks a gap in a field.
Through its glassless window
I watch the grass where a black goat stands
to look at the wind only goats can see.

The door frames an inner world.
Rust flecks its handle, the gleam gone from it.
Easy at last, I measure fields in light
that falls with forgiveness everywhere.

The Argument

1

I face again the disappointment
of things pushed from their proper place:
the dry flowers in an old basket,
the photograph of a poet's home,
the eggs carved from cherry wood
and set in a bowl near the door,
the smell of you on a damp towel.
It all comes down in the end to these.

2

I would sing this if it had an air,
a theme I know from other times.
Hurt becomes habit and I reach
for rhetoric, the steel phrase,
but end with hands against my face
rocking in silence as you turn your head,
continents away in the same bed.

3

I want to walk with you in Bohernabreena
in the cold days after Christmas when dogs
yap towards weirs and the stiff trees
are iced with frost. It is years ago
and before us the future flows like smooth
water falling with the semblance of silk.

4

A brief moon above a country road.
A song heard once on a late-night channel.
Blackberries uneaten in a narrow lane.

The Healing Island

My baggage rests on the quayside:
warm clothes for a week of winds,
notebooks for words that twitch
like a stick gripped above water.

❖

A pyramid of turf in the grate.
Sparks spit and flutter in a chimney
wide enough to inhale my cares,
hoovering them with a fierce *whoosh*.

❖

Mountains on the mainland fade
as rain clouds settle and swell.
Twelve summits disappear,
apostles assumed into skies and stars.

❖

Silence in a children's burial ground.
I stop among souls that have not been
hearing on wires a message from Limbo.
Stones are scattered like broken toys.

❖

I am missing you and long to tell
of fissures in cracked stone,
dragonflies on a well's skin,
filaments where prisms form.

❖

To pass you with your red hair
would draw bad luck to a boat.
Sooner turn back than risk such loss
though mackerel teem in a sunlit sea.

❖

There is news of a corncrake heard
among fields at the island's edge.
The story spreads in shops and lanes,
a hectic rumour of salvation.

❖

Night is closing like a claw
on islands where monks prayed.
Across hillsides pocked with warrens
gusts gather the gist of psalms.

❖

Woken by roosters, I reach
for my one book and find it dull.
No page seems equal to the deep
implosions of waves in coves.

❖

Minnows dart across pools
quicker than thoughts in my head.
I crave the stillness of water:
depths clear and surface sure.

❖

Striations on stones, the worn
force of centuries and the sea.
The thought of you as I work:
a glacier shifting earth's shape.

❖

Smell of turfsmoke on island paths,
stink of crab claws in a ditch.
Reek of oil in a trawler's hold,
odour of wax in a Sunday chapel.

❖

Flowers teem on ditch and wall.
Packed as mussels, firm petals part.
Frail stems teach the most:
thin as tissue, they outlast gales.

❖

In a dream our hands meet,
fingers splayed starfish.
Your cries rise with the cries
of kittiwakes on sheer cliffs.

❖

How to crack the cotton code
of sheets billowing on lines?
From the pier they seem a signal
inviting love to the far homes.

❖

An empty school faces the sea,
models askew in windows:
plasticine huts in a chalk quiet,
a playground empty of cries.

❖

I phone you from a call box,
windows misted and scratched.
Tones sound in an empty house,
a fact more bleak than gull's call.

❖

Columns of geese straddle the road.
The erect leader turns left,
leading his squadron to rock pools
where they drink: sentries at ease.

❖

Sheared sheep tremble in folds,
shreds of fleece catch in barbs.
Nets rot in an outhouse.
Hens lay in a rusted car.

❖

Wisps of bog cotton on a hill,
wisps of wool near a saint's well,
wisps of smoke from a chimney:
wisps of words to weave new ways.

❖

I remember being with you here:
red hair against white sand,
your black swimsuit among waves
striking as a glimpsed seal.

❖

Neighbours' gifts: a creel of turf,
white eggs in a cardboard box,
a saucepan of cooked claws,
mackerel wet from the bay.

❖

I gather shells from Duach beach.
Tiny as worries, they fill my palms.
The sea gives and neighbours give:
I open and yield to kindness.

❖

Let me cradle your head with my arm
and whisper love poems, secrets.
Your hands in mine are loved.
Mine in yours are held in turn.

❖

Before leaving I climb the mountain.
High among sheep and bladed winds,
I add my stone to the peak's cairn
and another for you: a summit reached.

Afterwords

He would not be fifty, if he were still alive — and he is ten years dead.

Seán Dunne was born in Waterford City in 1956. His mother, Maureen, died when she was thirty-three and Seán was four, the oldest of four children. A memoir, *In My Father's House* (1991, Gallery 2000), recorded the trials and tests of his childhood and the heroic roles enacted by his father, Richie, and their housekeeper, Tessie. Through the lens of personal experience it recreated the social history of a housing estate affectionately called John's Park. He published a pamphlet of poems, *Lady in Stone*, in 1975 or 1976 (his scrapbooks note both dates). Subsequently he published three collections, *Against the Storm* (Dolmen, 1985) and — with The Gallery Press — *The Sheltered Nest* (1992) and *Time and the Island* (1996) which he submitted two weeks before his death in Cork on 3 August 1995. In 1994 he published another prose book, *The Road to Silence* (New Island), 'an Irish spiritual odyssey'. He edited various anthologies including *Poets of Munster* (1985), *The Cork Anthology* (1993) and *Something Understood* (1995). A graduate of UCC, he made Cork his home where, from 1986, he worked as features writer and literary editor of *The Cork Examiner* and where he lived with his wife, Sara, and their three children, and, afterwards, with his partner, Trish, his children and her son.

Inevitably, the cornerstones of this book are the three published collections. To these I added fugitive pieces, some of which didn't seem at home in individual volumes at the time, and others which emerged from a trawl of Seán's notebooks and The Gallery Press archive. I resisted temptations to delete some poems from Seán's first collection. I restored dedications found in periodicals and manuscripts. I have included also a number of translations and his 'Letter from Ireland', one of whose various versions appeared in *Krino* (edited by Gerald Dawe) in 1989.

Seán practised translation as an ongoing part of his self-teaching. On 7 June 1992 he wrote 'I have some translations, which I'll send you on in time, including a long one of Valéry's "Cemetery by the Sea".' That never came, and I can find no trace of it, but I've included two translations from Irish originals, one verse, the other from the prose martyrology of Tallaght. I have included also a substantial selection of his versions of Anna Akhmatova (1899-1966).

Seán's social conscience was honed early. He wrote the title poem of *Against the Storm* in the wake of the murder of Archbishop Oscar Romero in El Salvador in March 1980, and it's little wonder he found a correspondence for his sense of the necessity of poetry in the dignified courage of the Russian writer. Isaiah Berlin, who met Akhmatova in Moscow in 1946, described her 'Requiem' as 'an elegy for Europe'. Seán's discursive 'Letter from Ireland' is, in certain ways, an elegy for his native land, its customs and decaying values. He found in Akhmatova's work a kind of Stations of the Cross, a record of the torment of the individuals who make up a nation. Every day for seventeen months Akhmatova queued outside the prison, where her son had been incarcerated in the Stalinist 'purges', and waited among the women who clutched their parcels for their husbands, sons and brothers, the women whose voice she vouched to become.

But if Seán's education included an immersion in other languages and literatures he was attracted and attentive, too, to the lessons of other cultures — from those of ancient Japan and China to those of the Shakers and the Jews. His were enduring themes — a concern with artifice (there are homages to artists and craftspeople in each of his books), spiritual sources and searches, from 'Morning at Mount Melleray' in *Against the Storm* to the final poem, 'The Healing Island', in his posthumous collection. He reprises the courtly ritual and ceremony of 'The Bluebell Ring' in many of his mature poems. The 'Emigrant Sheds, Cork' and 'Refugees' of his first book reappear in 'Refugees at Cobh' and 'Throwing the Beads'.

West Cork and its *gaeltacht* permeate his poetry and inform his later thinking.

Increasingly, Seán sought a core of belief in the 'conjunction of faith and intelligence' (a phrase he used about the writings of John Henry Newman). He worked towards a honed silence and learned both its values and its qualities. His hungers found sustenance in places — Mount Melleray, West Cork (Ballyvourney, the Beara Peninsula) and the West of Ireland, and Saint Gervais in Paris — as well as in the writings of Thomas Merton, Wendell Berry and Simone Weil. He rediscovered a particular solace in the Christian tradition. On 30 September 1979 he went to Knock to see the Pope. His comprehension of religion as an interior experience allowed the wisdom that prayer and contemplation without kind actions were like 'a song without a singer'.

One of the facts that made Seán Dunne's early death so sore a loss, in purely literary terms, is that, as the progress of this book demonstrates, his work was growing at once more pure and stronger. Early set pieces give way to distinctive, original poetry. The inevitable ventriloquism of, say, 'Doorsteps' — part Dylan Thomas, part Leonard Cohen — conceded to his own, earned voice. And a reason for this, I dare say, is that, as assiduously and as astutely as he studied the ways and workings of other poems, he was studying, and steadying, himself. An entry in his notebooks (1979) realizes 'for too long I fell into rhetoric. Now I want only to celebrate sunlight by telling how it was'. How good a poet he would have become we can only guess. What we can tell already and for sure is such work as his is worth attending to.

The following appeared in Seán's collections as dedications: 'for Sara' (*Against the Storm*), 'for Trish Edelstein' (*Time and the Island*); and as epigraphs: Hölderlin's 'But where there is danger there grows also what saves' (*Against the Storm*), the introductory lines Akhmatova added to her 'Requiem' (*The*

Sheltered Nest), and Muriel Rukeyser's 'It isn't that one brings life together — it's that one will not allow it to be torn apart' (*Time and the Island*).

Grateful acknowledgements are due to the editors and publishers of poems in this book. We appreciate also the help and encouragements, in various ways, of Phyllis Doolan, Tim Engelland, Stephen Enniss and his colleagues in Special Collections of the Robert W Woodruff Library at Emory University, Tom McCarthy and Catherine Coakley, and Colin Smythe. Trish Edelstein's enthusiastic responses and support have been a bonus and a pleasure. She immediately approved when I proposed the dedication to this book, believing also that it would have Seán's blessing.

Peter Fallon,
November 2005